GELATO FIASCO

GELATO FIASCO

Recipes and Stories from America's Best Gelato Makers

Joshua Davis
Bruno Tropeano
and
Cynthia Finnemore Simonds

Down East Books
CAMDEN, MAINE

DownEast Books

Published by Down East Books
An imprint of The Rowman & Littlefield Publishing Group, Inc.
4501 Forbes Blvd., Ste. 200
Lanham, MD 20706
www.rowman.com

Distributed by NATIONAL BOOK NETWORK

Copyright © 2018 by Gelato Fiasco
Photographs © 2018 by Jessica Keener Photography

Designed by Lynda Chilton, Chilton Creative

British Library Cataloguing-in-Publication Information available

Library of Congress Cataloging-in-Publication Data available

ISBN 978-1-60893-996-1 (hardcover)
ISBN 978-1-60893-997-8 (e-book)

∞™ The paper used in this publication meets the minimum requirements of American National Standard for Information Sciences—Permanence of Paper for Printed Library Materials, ANSI/NISO Z39.48-1992.

Printed in the United States of America.

*This cookbook
is dedicated to our
customers and our
employees—past, present,
and future.
You've each played a part
to make this wild dream
possible. We'll always be
eternally grateful.*

THE · GELA

FOREWORD

In Italy the best *gelaterias* make gelato every day using local milk, the finest ingredients available, and traditional techniques perfected centuries ago.

But alas! . . . something tragic happened as Italy's sweetest treasure found its way to America. So-called "gelato" started popping up here and there, but most were made with little respect for the art of gelato. Bland, pre-made, and over-iced, these impostors started to be passed off as "gelato." The traditions that made the frozen treat a delight were beginning to be lost.

Until now.

Inspired by tales of gelato past, and following in the footsteps of the *gelatieri* before us, we set out to rediscover the techniques and practices of the Old World Italian masters of gelato and use them as a foundation for creating new American flavors born of the essential traits of truly artisanal gelato—using locally sourced milk, adding only the best ingredients, and making a fresh product daily.

Gelato Fiasco is the result of our quest.

We're proud to bring to you the best gelato made anywhere. If you don't agree, please let us know and we'll make it right.

—Bruno & Josh, Gelatieri

INTRODUCTION

One of the most interesting phenomenons about being a gelato maker is having people apologize when they refer to your craft as "ice cream." It happens to me constantly. People will say to me, "Hey Josh, I stopped by your shop and had some of your delicious ice cre . . . um . . . gelato!"

I have considered this phenomenon over the last several years and actually appreciate exactly the origin of this freudian slip—first of all, gelato *is* ice cream in Italy. In Rome, if you say to your friends, "Let's go get ice cream," they assume you mean gelato. If you meant American-style ice cream, your Italian friends would probably just stay home. However, in Brunswick, Maine, (where I typically have this conversation) gelato *and* ice cream are available. Gelato Fiasco has made gelato just as approachable as ice cream; in its proper place as just one of dozens of styles of frozen desserts we all enjoy. That's something I am proud of! So, I choose to assume that's what people mean when they say they love my "ice cream."

SO WHAT MAKES GELATO DIFFERENT ANYWAY?

Most people know that gelato is a style of ice cream that dates back several centuries to Italy. Gelato is different from American-style ice cream basically because of two things: butterfat and density. Gelato is denser (meaning it has less air in it) and is made with milk as the first ingredient, instead of cream. This means it has a lower butterfat content, giving gelato a wonderfully dense texture that is not dominated by the flavor of butterfat. The flavors come through cleanly, with more range of expression on the palate than traditional ice cream.

The intensity of flavor and the density make gelato's texture the thing that people write home about. Anyone who has tried gelato knows what I mean—a dense, pudding-like quality that is just different than ice cream. There are all kinds of scientific implications of the lower density in terms of impact on other qualities of the gelato, but just know that density is good and key to excellent gelato.

GELATO IN THE WORLD TODAY

Today, gelato around the world is of varying qualities. They are highly dependent upon whether the dessert is made from scratch or by mixing milk with pre-made powders, mixes, or gels; the skill of the person creating the gelato; and the quality of the ingredients used. No matter where you are, using fresh, whole ingredients is the key to making a great product. We're so lucky here in Maine. We know the farmers who raise the cows that provide the milk that makes our gelato. Trust me, these are some happy cows! Starting from scratch, Bruno put his mad scientist skills to work developing formulas to make a perfect batch of gelato every time. In each of our stores, the gelato is made fresh every day. Around the world, gelato shops are in one of two categories: those who make gelato from milk and a mix, and those who make gelato from scratch. The former is more common, but the latter tastes better every time!

HOW DID GELATO FIASCO COME INTO BEING?

I met Bruno my freshman year in college in 2001. He was friends with one of my fourth floor-mates and I clearly remember my first conversation with him. "So is your name really Bruno?" He was wearing gold chains, had a very imposing physical presence, and had a personality to match. We quickly hit it off. He was witty, we had a common love of *Star Trek: The Next Generation* and he seemed like an interesting guy to get to know.

Our first business together was a blackjack table we ran out of our dorm room. In the interest of avoiding self-incrimination, I won't go into detail, except to say we liked working together. We started to look for more opportunities and soon enough, another chance presented itself.

We spent the next two years going to college full-time and building and selling a nine lot subdivision in Maine. By the time we were seniors, we had built a successful business and we knew what our post-college plans would be. Also, during this time, Bruno met a girl and planned to move to Maine after college. He decided to buy a duplex in Rome, Maine, and asked if I wanted to rent a room from him. So, in May 2005, Bruno and I, both graduated and ready for the next step in our business lives, found ourselves living in Rome.

We still laugh at the irony that Rome, Maine was the birthplace of our gelato business. The very first inkling of the idea came as a result in a downturn in the real estate business. We had noticed that it was taking longer and longer to sell our properties and became worried that the boom was over. We started looking for our next act. We decided that we wanted to work together on something new and began using our increasing free time to brainstorm the possibilities.

The leading idea was a microbrewery, but we doubted we had enough capital to get it up and running. Our runner-up was a specialty food grocery store and take-out meal bar. This was pre-Whole Foods in Maine, before we had ever set foot in one of their stores. However, our idea was basically a small scale version of a Whole Foods Store. We would offer gelato in our store, and that was how the first seed was planted.

When Bruno's parents came to visit, we told them our new idea. Bruno's mom liked the idea for the gelato bar, but she thought we should forget about the rest of it and just open a gelato shop.

"There are 30 million people in Italy and about a million gelato shops. In the United States there are 300 million people and no gelato shops." With those words, it became crystal clear to both of us that gelato was our future.

For the first step we signed up for a two-day class in New York City and got a basic introduction to the art of making gelato. It was taught by Luciano Ferrari, a leading gelato educator from Italy, but it featured gelato made with pastes and powders from the industrial suppliers in Italy and only briefly touched on how to make gelato from scratch. Despite that, we were hooked. This was the first time I had ever made gelato or had it straight from the batch freezer. I was stunned with how delicious gelato could be.

While we were in New York City, we decided to check out the other gelato shops in the area. Keep in mind, this was before gelato had achieved any level of awareness to the mainstream American consumer. When we told our friends why we were in New York City, they not only questioned our sanity but didn't even know what gelato was. Telling them that it was a style of ice cream didn't help assuage their concern for our future. There were not many gelato shops anywhere in the U.S. Ciao

Bella and Labortorio del Gelato are two I remember from New York City. Everywhere we visited that had a gelato case gave us an immediate sense of the opportunity—if we could pull it off.

> *Gelato was still something exotic,*
> *something that people you knew who had*
> *been to Italy would rave about.*

The leading contender for the name of our business was The Gelato Fiasco. It sounded memorable and ridiculous and we were sure it would attract attention, but we knew it needed a hook if it was going to work.

MILK FROM FAMILY FARMS

We source 100% of our whole milk and cream from family dairy farms. As far as we know, we're one of the few ice cream or gelato companies with national distribution to source 100% of its milk from nearby farms, and offer transparent information about milk sources. It costs a little more to operate this way and poses some logistical challenges, but we wouldn't make any other choice. All of our farms pledge not to use artificial growth hormones. Our milk commitment means that we're not only supporting the farms that are important to Maine's culture, economy, and landscape, but that we're also using what we believe is the richest, freshest milk in America (maybe we believe that because we grew up drinking it). We hope you can taste the difference!

Then I had a brainstorm: What if the distinctive gelato spoons were crossed like an X on a treasure map. We'd have custom red palettini spoons made and we could make up a treasure map. The map would lead to the treasure that is incredible gelato. I mocked up some historical looking art with a red gelato spoon marking the treasure of the lost art of gelato. And the name The Gelato Fiasco referred to the time before we existed—before the lost art of gelato making had been rediscovered. Bruno loved it!

Our first order of pints was delivered in an Igloo cooler in the back of my Ford truck. I got paid in cash, said thanks, and then waited to see what happened. A few days later, he called me and I expected the worst. Did he want me to come pick up the pints? I was shocked when he nonchalantly said he needed to reorder. His reorder was double the number of pints of his first.

We knew that fundamentally, there are a lot of connections between the food culture in Maine and in Italy. Both celebrate the finest regional ingredients. We could take the best aspects of traditional Italian gelato: fresh, seasonal, local, and meld that foundation with the flavors, sensibilities, and culture of Maine. By using the best ingredients, especially local milk and cream, and making the flavors that appealed to our local tastes, we were doing exactly what they would do in Italy. Our brand would remain focused on creating the very best gelato from scratch, using local, fresh ingredients and be distinctive as a Maine gelato company—one that is inspired by Italy and perfected in Maine. That philosophy ultimately became our motto and is still how we view our world.

METHODS

How to Use this Cookbook

A RIGHT SMART AMOUNT

In the world of gelato making we rely on weights rather than volume measurements. Did you know 1 cup of cocoa weighs 3 ounces? 1 cup of flour and 1 cup of cocoa and 1 cup of milk all weigh different amounts. Think of a pound of rocks and a pound of feathers—very different in terms of actual mass. With that in mind, at Gelato Fiasco, and we believe at home, the only way to get a consistent result from a recipe is by accurate measurement of ingredients. Online and in stores you can find good digital kitchen scales for less than $10. Investing more than that in ingredients makes the scale the cheapest insurance policy you'll find. Once you get used to trusting weight as your measure, you'll get spectacular results that you can count on every time.

SIMPLE TO SNAZZY EQUIPMENT

Getting ready to make gelato, you'll need some basic tools and equipment in your kitchen. Sauce pans, whisks, spoons, and bowls are standard fare. A kitchen scale (we like digital), candy thermometer, and ice cream maker will take you to the brink of perfection. All you have to do is trust the recipes, follow the directions, and throw caution to the wind. We'll be rooting you on, hoping you post pictures of your triumphs on Instagram: @GelatoFiasco! Can't wait to see how your imagination transforms our creations!

BUILDING FLAVORS

All of our recipes in this book are scaled down to make it easy for you at home. They generally will fit in the bowl of a standard home ice cream maker. The recipes can be multiplied in most cases with great success. The bases are the foundations for creating extraordinary gelato. There are a few to choose from and the different flavors that follow all begin with one of the mother bases. Regardless of which one you choose, the base plus the flavor ingredients all need to be chilled completely before pouring them into your ice cream maker. If you have a kitchen thermometer, it's best to start with the base at 45 degrees or cooler. A cooled base will make freezing and churning a breeze. Depending on the machine it may take only 20 minutes to transform the liquid into frozen gelato deliciousness. In every case, you can eat the gelato right out of the machine or spoon it into sealable jars or containers and place it in the freezer to enjoy later.

FREEZING

The key to the freezing process is to freeze the mix as quickly as possible. Speed is your friend for two major reasons: 1) the quicker the freezing process the smaller the ice crystals that form. 2) less freezing time means there is less time for air to be incorporated into the mix. These are important when making ice cream but are critical when making gelato. Your tongue is a sophisticated tasting sensor which can detect ice crystals as small as 20 microns (.0008 inches!). If large crystals exist in the product it tastes icy, gritty, sandy, or coarse. If there is too much air than the product will taste fluffy and possibly flat—more like whipped cream instead delicious gelato. In our shops we use

FLAVOR ALERTS

One of the tough things about having made more than 1,500 flavors over ten years—but only 40 flavors on any given day—is that invariably, somebody always wants a flavor that isn't there that moment! We came up with several ways to help smooth out this problem.

First, almost since the beginning, we've posted the daily flavors to our website every morning. Later, we worked with a computer programmer to create a system called Flavor Alerts. People can register for the alerts and then we email them the moment it's made! Lots of people subscribe to this service, and we like to think we're the only gelato shop in the world that offers this.

Finally, each week, we create a special Featured Flavor—something especially seasonal, fun, or interesting—that we share with our Facebook and Instagram followers. By featuring it for a week, customers can be sure that they'll be able to find it. All these tools allow us to combine spur-of-the-moment surprises with reliable processes that customers can trust; that's the sweet spot of hospitality.

fancy machines to ensure the freezing happens as quickly as possible. A gallon of mix and be frozen in as little as 6 minutes. At home this is usually not possible—it usually takes about 30. So it's critical to keep all the ingredients and parts as cold as you can get them. Each flavor element should be chilled before it is incorporated into the base.

A WORD ABOUT SUGAR

Sugar in gelato not only provides the sweetness necessary to qualify as dessert, sugar is also critical to achieving right texture. Sugar depresses the freezing point of water and helps keep some of it unfrozen, so the final product has the incredible texture we associate with great gelato. If you add too much sugar, not only will the final taste be too sweet, it will have a coarse and sandy texture. If you don't have enough sugar in the mixture, the final texture will be icy or too hard. Balancing the right amount of sugar, so the right amount of water remains unfrozen, is a science because sugar comes into the recipe via two ways: what you scoop in yourself and what is present in the ingredients you are adding. If you're using molasses or honey as flavoring, you need to account for that and reduce the amount of sugar you add to the base. Another complication comes from using fruit. All fruit has varying amounts of both sugar and water which need to be considered. We have determined the proper amounts of each to add to the recipe to perfectly balance the sugar and water, to achieve the best consistency and right amount of sweetness.

Honey, maple syrup, agave nectar, and other liquid sugars don't work well in place of sugar in gelato recipes and can't be used as a substitute cup for cup. Their place in the gelato maker's pantry is as a flavoring not solely as a sweetener.

And in case you're wondering: Not all sugar is created equal. You'll find corn syrup and sugar alcohols in a lot of frozen desserts. Corn syrup is a really helpful (albeit probably unfairly controversial) ingredient in the gelato maker's pantry. It delivers about 80% of the sweetness of regular white cane sugar, but depresses the freezing point in a similar way and actually provides superior texture support for a better mouth-feel. We don't generally use corn syrup at the shop because of its bad rap, but do draw a very hard line at using high fructose corn syrup. It deserves all of its negative attention for being unnatural and highly processed. We do like good old corn syrup for home use. My grandmother certainly loved using it and I don't see any reason we should treat the juice from cane plants any different than the juice from corn plants.

Fake sugars, sugar alcohols, etc.? Just don't.

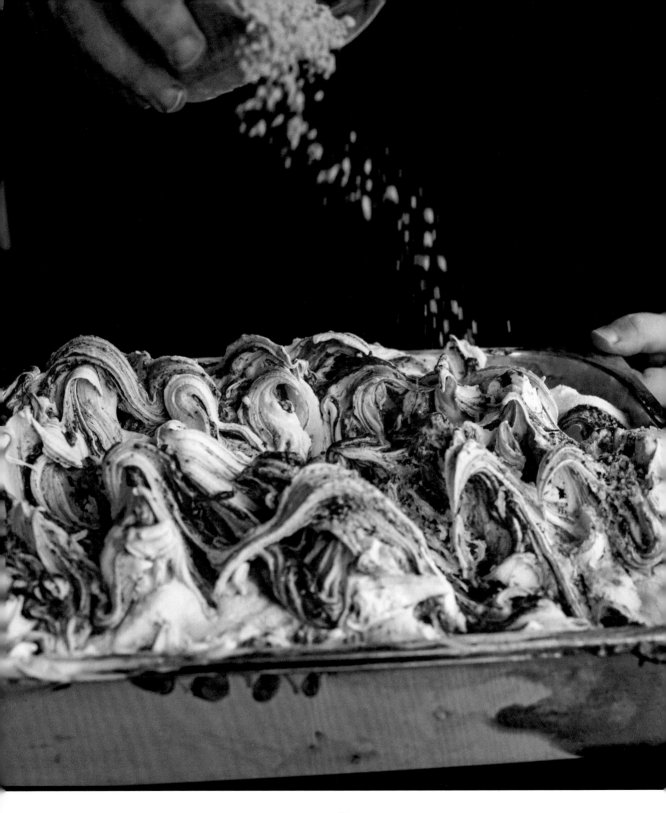

INCLUSIONS, CHUNKS, AND SWIRLS

When anything is folded, swirled, stirred, or incorporated into a gelato base, it is called an inclusion. The timing of this addition has a great impact on the finished product. After freezing, according to your machine's directions, it is time to take out the gelato. If it is a smooth flavor such as Strawberry Balsamic, with no chunks, it is done. Move the finished gelato to an airtight container and store in the freezer.

If it is a chunky flavor, like Cookie Therapy, then you need to fold in the chopped cookie pieces. After you chop the inclusion into bite-sized pieces put it in a bowl in the freezer. It is important that the inclusion is as cold as possible since you will be adding it to frozen gelato. If the inclusion is even room temperature as it hits the frozen gelato, it melts some, and can cause ice crystals to form.

There are some home machines that allow you to add inclusions during the freezing process. You will want to do this as close to the end as possible. You don't want the machine to mash the chunks and transform the pieces into gelato that is still fairly smooth or have it frozen improperly. If you can't add the inclusions into the machine, another way to get those chunks into the gelato is to put the finished gelato into a chilled stainless steel bowl and manually mix them in yourself. Speed, as always, will be your friend here. Chill the inclusion (chunky bits) while the gelato churns, then pour whatever you're adding right onto the gelato and fold them together with a metal gelato spade (also chilled). Once they are mixed, put the finished chunky gelato into an airtight container and get it in the freezer.

REAL FRUITS, NUTS, AND CONFECTIONS

It's pretty simple: We find the best ingredients and use them. That's why our flavors are so delicious, and why we feel good about serving them. We get pistachios from Sicily, vanilla beans from Madagascar, and wild blueberries from down the coast. The candies that we use have their own special category—they may use a preservative or two in their formula. When you buy one of our pints from the grocery store (sans candy), you can be confident that it does not contain any artificial flavors.

Recipes From the
Gelato Fiasco Vault

Gelato Mother Bases

When making mother bases, be sure the base and machine parts are as cold as possible. The quicker the machine freezes the mix the better it will be. Gelato is best eaten immediately, on its own or with your favorite toppings. To save for later, pack frozen gelato in an airtight container or spoon into three pint-sized canning jars with lids and store in the freezer.

⟨RICH YELLOW GELATO BASE⟩

Gloriously rich, liquid gold custard is the first base to master in your gelato repertoire. Its versatility allows you to elevate any gelato to stellar heights. The Rich Yellow Gelato Base can be substituted for the Classic White Gelato Base in any of the following recipes if you're in the mood for a custard-y variation.

INGREDIENTS:

¼ cup (2 oz. or 72g) heavy cream

3 cups (25½ oz. or 750g) whole milk

1¼ cup (8½ oz. or 240g) sugar

2⅛ cups (2¼ oz. or 63g) skim milk powder

1 teaspoon (4g) sea salt

10 egg yolks (5 oz. or 142g)

In a medium-sized pot, combine the cream, milk, sugar, skim milk powder, and salt over low heat. Gently bring the mixture up to a simmer, whisking to incorporate all of the ingredients. Cook until the sugar and skim milk powder dissolve completely. This should take about 5 minutes, once the mixture has started simmering. Remove the pot from the heat.

In a separate bowl, whisk the egg yolks for about 30 seconds, until they are homogenous.

While constantly whisking (so that the eggs don't cook), slowly pour about a third of the hot cream mixture into the yolks. Then, carefully but quickly, whisk the yolk mixture back into the pot with the remaining cream.

Return the pot to the heat and turn the burner to medium-low. Keep an eye on the mixture and continue to stir with a spoon instead of the whisk (no need to be too vigorous — you are just trying to keep the mixture moving). Once the mixture is thick enough to coat the back of a spoon, which will be about 180 degrees F on an instant-read thermometer — you will be ready to strain it.

Pour the mixture through a fine mesh strainer into a bowl. Cool to room temperature as fast as possible and then cover and chill in the refrigerator for at least 4 hours or overnight.

If you just can't wait, you can pour the warm mixture into a zip top freezer bag. With the bag securely sealed, submerge the liquid into a large bowl filled with ice water. Manipulate the liquid (squish it around) so it cools quickly. Pour out some of the water and add more ice to the bowl as the water bath warms. For us, this took about 25 minutes.

Once the base has chilled, churn it in your home ice cream maker according to the manufacturer's instructions.

Yield: 42 oz. (about 3 pints).

⸑ DECADENT CHOCOLATE GELATO BASE ⸒

This silky chocolate concoction is essentially a cocoa infused creme anglaise. In liquid form, we heat it and serve as our luxurious sipping chocolate. Chilled, it can be blended with ice or frozen cubes of espresso, coffee, or chocolate milk to make a frosty frappe of sorts—a frozen hot chocolate. Then of course, churned into gelato, it's the perfect base for many of our chocolate flavors. With minor changes, it becomes Big County Brownie, Dark Chocolate Sea Salt Caramel, Hazelnut Dark Chocolate, and more. So simple, so versatile, so delicious.

INGREDIENTS:

¼ cup (2½ oz. or 72g) heavy cream

3 cups (25½ oz. or 750g) whole milk

1¼ cups (8½ oz. or 240g) sugar

1¼ cups (3½ oz. or 100g) unsweetened cocoa powder

1½ teaspoons (6g) sea salt

6 egg yolks (3 oz. or 85g)

In a medium-sized pot, combine the cream, milk, sugar, cocoa powder, and salt over low heat. Gently bring the mixture up to a simmer, whisking to incorporate all of the ingredients. Cook until the sugar and cocoa powder dissolve completely. This should take about 5 minutes, once the mixture has started simmering. Remove the pot from the heat.

In a separate bowl, whisk the egg yolks for about 30 seconds, until they are homogenous.

While constantly whisking (so that the eggs don't cook), slowly pour about a third of the hot cream mixture into the yolks. Then, carefully but quickly, whisk the yolk mixture back into the pot with the remaining cream.

Return the pot to the heat and turn the burner to medium-low. Keep an eye on the mixture and continue to stir with a spoon instead of the whisk (no need to be too vigorous—you are just trying to keep the mixture moving). Once the mixture is thick enough to coat the back of a spoon—which will be about 180 degrees on an instant-read thermometer—you will be ready to strain it.

Pour the mixture through a fine mesh strainer into a bowl. Cool to room temperature as fast as possible and then cover and chill in the refrigerator for at least 4 hours or overnight.

If you just can't wait, you can pour the warm mixture into a zip top freezer bag. With the bag securely sealed, submerge the liquid into a large bowl filled with ice water. Manipulate the liquid (squish it around) so it cools quickly. Pour out some of the water and add more ice as the water bath warms. For us, this took about 25 minutes.

Once the base has chilled, churn it in your home ice cream maker according to the manufacturer's instructions.

Yield: 42 oz. base (about 3 pints).

MILK CHOCO-LIGHT GELATO BASE

For those who crave milk chocolate, this base will fit the bill. Lighter chocolate than our decadent base, it is rich and full of milk chocolate flavor. Perfect if you'd like to enjoy the sweeter side of the chocolate continuum.

INGREDIENTS:

½ cup (5 oz. or 145g) heavy cream

3 cups (25½ oz. or 750g) whole milk

1¼ cups (8½ oz. or 240g) sugar

1¼ cups (3½ oz. or 100g) unsweetened cocoa powder

½ cup (1 oz. or 28g) skim milk powder

1½ teaspoons (6g) sea salt

4 egg yolks (2 oz. or 85g)

In a medium-sized pot, combine the cream, milk, sugar, cocoa powder, skim milk powder, and salt over low heat.

Gently bring the mixture up to a simmer, whisking to incorporate all of the ingredients. Cook until the sugar and skim milk powder dissolve completely. This should take about 5 minutes, once the mixture has started simmering. Remove the pot from the heat.

In a separate bowl, whisk the egg yolks for about 30 seconds, until they are homogenous.

While constantly whisking (so that the eggs don't cook), slowly pour about a third of the hot cream mixture into the yolks. Then, carefully but quickly, whisk the yolk mixture back into the pot with the remaining cream.

Return the pot to the heat and turn the burner to medium-low. Keep an eye on the mixture and continue to stir with a spoon instead of the whisk (no need to be too vigorous — you are just trying to keep the mixture moving). Once the mixture is thick enough to coat the back of a spoon — which will be about 180 degrees F on an instant-read thermometer — you will be ready to strain it.

Pour the mixture through a fine mesh strainer into a bowl. Cool to room temperature as fast as possible and then cover and chill in the refrigerator for at least 4 hours or overnight.

If you just can't wait, you can pour the warm mixture into a zip top freezer bag. With the bag securely sealed, submerge the liquid into a large bowl filled with ice water. Manipulate the liquid (squish it around) so it cools quickly. Pour out some of the water and add more ice to the bowl as the water bath warms. For us, this took about 25 minutes.

Once the base has chilled, churn it in your home ice cream maker according to the manufacturer's instructions.

Yield: 42 oz. (about 3 pints).

MAKING GELATO AT HOME
WITHOUT AN ICE CREAM MACHINE

If you don't have an ice cream machine you can still make gelato at home. It may not have exactly the same texture since it will not be churned as it's frozen, but the flavors and richness will make for a nice dessert. To give it a go:

Clear a flat space in your freezer where you can set a loaf pan or two mason jars without touching other frozen items. When your gelato mixture is made, pour it into the loaf pan or mason jars, cover and place it in the refrigerator for two hours. After it has cooled, place your container(s) in the freezer. Set a timer for thirty minutes. When thirty minutes have elapsed, take the container(s) of gelato out of the freezer. Scrape down the sides of the container(s) and stir for one minute. Cover and place it back in the freezer. Continue to stir the gelato every thirty minutes for four hours. At this point the gelato should be the consistency of thick yogurt. Cover it and allow it to freeze for another two hours or overnight undisturbed; then it's ready to serve. Your gelato can be stored for up to a week in the freezer.

❧ CLASSIC WHITE GELATO BASE ❧
AKA FRESH CREAM GELATO

When we first opened, we tended to mix traditional Italian names for flavors with English names. There wasn't a cohesive naming style for our shops yet, which would come in 2012. So, this flavor's original name was "Fior di latte" or "flower of the milk." It's a beautiful, descriptive name for just the taste of fresh milk and cream.

To make gelato egg free we use guar gum, a naturally derived thickener found in the gluten free baking area of your favorite grocery store. It is used in many products to keep baked goods, desserts and yes, gelato, thick and stable with fewer ice crystals. It's just another way to make creamy frozen desserts without using eggs.

INGREDIENTS:

½ cup cream (5 oz. or 145g)

3 cups whole milk (25½ oz. or 750g)

⅞ cup skim milk powder (2 oz. or 56g)

1 teaspoon sea salt (4g)

1 cup sugar (8 oz. or 227g)

1 teaspoon (2g) guar gum or 3 egg yolks
   (1½ oz. or 42g)

In a small bowl thoroughly combine the ⅓ of the sugar and guar gum powder. Or if using eggs, in a small bowl whisk the yolks and ⅓ of the sugar until the mixture is homogenous.

In a medium pot, combine cream, milk, skim milk powder, remaining two-thirds of the sugar, and salt over low heat. Slowly whisk the sugar and guar gum into the milk while it's still cool. (OR, If you prefer to use eggs to thicken the base, while constantly whisking [so that the eggs don't cook], slowly pour about a third of the hot cream mixture into the yolks and sugar mixture. Then, carefully but quickly, whisk the yolk mixture back into the pot with the remaining cream.)

Gently bring the mixture up to a simmer, whisking often to incorporate all of the ingredients. Cook until the sugar and skim milk powder dissolve completely. This should take about 5 minutes. Turn the burner to medium-low. Keep an eye on the mixture and continue to stir with a spoon instead of the whisk (no need to be too vigorous—you are just trying to keep the mixture moving). Once the mixture is thick enough to coat the back of a spoon—which will be about 180 degrees on an instant-read thermometer—you will be ready to strain it.

Pour the mixture through a fine mesh strainer into a bowl. Cool to room temperature as fast as possible and then cover and chill in the refrigerator for at least 4 hours or overnight.

If you just can't wait, you can pour the warm mixture into a zip top freezer bag. Carefully seal the bag and removing as much air as you can. With the bag securely sealed, submerge the liquid into a large bowl filled with ice water. Manipulate the liquid (squish it around) so it cools quickly. Pour out some of the water and add more ice to the bowl as the water bath warms. For us, this took about 25 minutes.

Once the base has chilled, churn it in your home ice cream maker according to the manufacturer's instructions.

Yield: 45 oz. (about 3 pints).

● ●

❧VEGAN COCONUT BASE❧

If you're looking for a rich, dairy-free gelato, this coconut base gives you decadent options. You can substitute it in any of the recipes that follow. Keep in mind that you may want to adjust the sweetness to suit your fancy. We use Goya brand coconut milk and coconut cream. It has the perfect amount of fat to sugar ratio that makes this recipe work. If you can't find Goya you may need to add a bit more coconut cream or coconut oil to give it the same creamy texture.

INGREDIENTS:

1 can (13½ oz. or 375g) Goya coconut milk

⅔ cup (5 oz. or 145g) Goya coconut cream

1 tablespoon (½ oz. or 14g) coconut oil

1¾ cups (14 oz. or 400g) water

1 teaspoon (4g) sea salt

1 cup (8 oz. or 227g) sugar

½ teaspoon (2g) guar gum

In a medium-sized pot, combine the coconut milk, coconut cream, coconut oil, water, salt, and sugar over low heat. Gently bring the mixture up to a simmer, whisking to incorporate all of the ingredients. Cook until the sugar and coconut oil dissolve completely. Sprinkle guar gum over the top of the mixture and stir in. Continue to whisk until all ingredients are thoroughly incorporated. This should take about 5 minutes, once the mixture has started simmering. Remove the pot from the heat.

Once the mixture is thick enough to coat the back of a spoon- which will be about 180 degrees on an instant read thermometer- you'll be ready to strain it. Pour the mixture through a fine mesh strainer into a bowl. Cool to room temperature as fast as possible and then cover and chill in the refrigerator for at least 4 hours or overnight.

Once the base has chilled, churn it in your home ice cream maker according to the manufacturer's instructions.

Yield: 36 oz. (about 2 pints).

❧ SORBETTO BASE ☙
AKA SUGAR BASE

When making fruit sorbetto, make sure your fresh fruit is as ripe as possible. Riper fruit tastes sweeter and blends more easily. Some fruit are more easily incorporated cooked than raw, Apples, for instance, are often added as cooked applesauce to the gelato base. One easy way to have ingredients ready at home: when bananas start to brown or berries start to soften, peel or hull them and place the fruit in a zip top plastic bag. Remove as much air as possible from the bag and seal it. Place the sealed bag on the counter and flatten it to leave a single layer of fruit. Place the bag in the freezer. Next time you're ready to make gelato, your super-ripe banana or berries will be recipe-ready!

INGREDIENTS:

1 lb (16 oz. or 454 g) very ripe fresh or frozen fruit, pureed

1 lb (16 oz. or 454 g) Sugar Syrup (see pg. 39)

1 cup (8 oz. or 227 g) water

2 tablespoons (½ oz. or 14 g) fresh lemon juice

Pinch of sea salt (2g)

Wash, dry and remove any peels, stems, leaves, pits or seeds from your fruit. Chop or cut your fruit into ¼-inch or 1 cm pieces. Using a food processor, blender or immersion blender puree the fruit and sugar syrup. Add the water, lemon juice and salt. Continue to blend until the mixture is silky smooth. Place the mixture into a covered container. Chill for 30 minutes or overnight.

Once the base has chilled, freeze it in your home ice cream maker according to the manufacturer's directions.

Yield: 40 oz. (about 3 pints).

Chunks are not your friends! They make for icy sorbetto! :(

Swirls, Variegates, Caramels, and Crisps

❦HOMEMADE CHOCOLATE TRUFFLES❦

These truffles are the perfect way to deliver delicious, soft chocolate chunks into your gelato. If you just throw in chocolate chips, they will be waxy when frozen and not deliver the right mouthfeel. These are super easy to make. Here is the size batch we make in the store. If you'd like a smaller quantity, feel free to halve or quarter the amounts for slightly less temptation.

NOTE: You'll need an instant read thermometer for tempering the chocolate in this recipe.

INGREDIENTS:

2⅔ cups (21 oz. or 595g) coconut oil

5¼ cups (42 oz. or 1190g) semisweet (or another other favorite type) chocolate, separated into two parts: 30 oz./850g and 12 oz./340g

1 teaspoon (5g) sea salt

Melt the coconut oil in a double boiler. Add half of the chocolate. While the chocolate is melting, stir occasionally until smooth. Bring the mixture to 114 degrees.

Remove from the heat and add in the remaining half of the chocolate. Stir continuously until the temperature comes down to 82 degrees. Move the top of the double boiler to a cool water bath if necessary to reduce the temperature. Stirring cools and promotes good crystal formation in the chocolate. (Be very careful-water and chocolate are not friends. If you get any water into the chocolate mixture, it may seize and become one unfortunate brown lump.)

Once the mixture reaches 82 degrees return it to the double boiler and continuously stir until it reaches 88 degrees. This process of heating and cooling and reheating the chocolate is called tempering. By tempering the chocolate, it will remain glossy and smooth without developing the whitish film seen when the fat separates. (This chocolate defect is called "blooming.")

We use this chocolate truffle recipe in several ways. One of the most popular is to cool the mixture until it is room temperature, but still liquid, and drizzle over a batch of gelato, breaking it up as it cools and solidifies. Another is to smooth it into a parchment or foil lined sheet pan and chill until firm. It can then be removed and chopped into chunks or bits for adding to your gelato.

Yield: 63 oz. (almost 4 lbs).

❧CARAMELS❧

Cooking the magical combination of sugar, water, cream, butter, salt, and vanilla will result in some kind of caramelly goodness. Depending on the amounts of those ingredients, the temperature, and duration of that heat, the caramel can run the gamut from pourable sauce to solid as a rock. Each of the following caramels fit in along the spectrum, each one different, all of them delicious!

CARAMEL FOR CARAMEL SEA SALT GELATO

Jumping on the salty caramel bandwagon, Bruno developed several caramels that stand up to the flavors they enhance. The first is a traditional sugar, cream and vanilla caramel. Adding salt to the gelato base prevents it from dissolving and getting lost in the flavors and keeps the little crunch that Caramel Sea Salt lovers enjoy. We suggest using a stainless steel or light colored saucepan in order to see the caramel change in color. Pots with a non-stick or black metal interior make it difficult to gauge the caramel's progress.

INGREDIENTS:

1 cup (8 oz. or 226g) white sugar

1 cup (8 oz. or 226g) heavy cream

1 teaspoon (5g) vanilla

In a large, deep, heavy-bottomed saucepan, spread the sugar in an even layer and place over low to medium low heat. Watch it carefully. Once it starts to liquefy around the edges, use a rubber spatula to very gently stir it towards the center. Continue gently stirring until all of the sugar is melted, but take care not to over stir.

When the caramel reaches a deep amber color, immediately remove it from the heat. Carefully whisk in half the cream, which will bubble and steam quite violently. Stir until the cream is thoroughly combined, then whisk in remaining cream. Stir in the vanilla. If any sugar has hardened, place the saucepan over low heat and whisk until smooth.

Yield: 16 oz.

Caramel for Dark Chocolate Caramel Sea Salt Gelato

This caramel is deep, golden and has the almost burnt sugar flavor that helps it match the intensity of dark chocolate in the Dark Chocolate Caramel Sea Salt Gelato. Make this caramel as your gelato base begins to cool. You'll want to stir it into the base while both parts are still warm. We suggest using a stainless steel or light colored saucepan in order to see the caramel change in color. Pots with a non-stick or black metal interior make it difficult to gauge the caramel's progress.

INGREDIENTS:

1 cup (8 oz. or 226g) sugar

In a large, deep, heavy-bottomed saucepan, spread the sugar in an even layer and place over low to medium low heat. Watch it carefully. Once it starts to liquefy around the edges, use a rubber spatula to very gently stir it towards the center. Continue gently stirring until all of the sugar is melted, but take care not to over stir. Once the caramel reaches a deep amber color, immediately remove it from the heat. Allow to cool for 5 minutes but you are going to want to use this in the chocolate base quickly as deep amber caramel hardens as it cools to room temperature. Be careful since it will still be hot.

Makes enough for one batch of gelato

Banana Caramel

Smooth, rich, and dotted with bursts of banana, this caramel is swirled into its partner gelato. The aroma of vanilla and banana together is reminiscent of old-fashioned banana cream pie found at every family event; it has always been a holiday favorite! Banana caramel is the perfect accompaniment! We suggest using a stainless steel or light colored saucepan in order to see the caramel change in color. Pots with a non-stick or black metal interior make it difficult to gauge the caramel's progress.

INGREDIENTS:

1 cup (8 oz. or 227g) white sugar

1 cup (8 oz. or 227g) heavy cream

2 teaspoons (10g) vanilla

1 banana, coarsely chopped

In a large, deep, heavy-bottomed saucepan, spread the sugar in an even layer and place over low to medium low heat. Watch it carefully. Once it starts to liquefy around the edges, use a rubber spatula to very gently stir it towards the center. Continue gently stirring until all of the sugar is melted, but take care not to over stir.

Once the caramel reaches a deep amber color, immediately remove it from the heat. Carefully whisk in half the cream, which will bubble and steam quite violently. Stir until the cream is thoroughly combined, then whisk in the remaining cream. Stir in the vanilla and banana. If any sugar has hardened, place the saucepan over low heat and whisk until smooth. Cool completely before adding to gelato.

Yield: 18 oz.

When we started Gelato Fiasco, we had very little experience with hiring employees or the rules surrounding labor laws, especially with minors. Since we opened during the summer vacation period, our younger employees could work more hours and we had the shop perfectly staffed. However, once the summer vacation ended, we reviewed the labor laws and realized that most of our staff would have much more limited availability than what they could and were willing to work and none could work late at night. Enter: Peter Beltramini to save the day. Peter was one of the few members of the staff who could legally work all of the hours the shop was open and he connected with customers. He's been a fixture of the staff ever since that first summer and you're sure to recognize Peter if you have ever visited the Brunswick shop.

Fruit Swirls or Fruit Variegate

At Gelato Fiasco, we call fruit additions to a recipe a variegate. It's just a technical term for a swirl. The variegates below use different amounts of sugar to best match the fruit in the recipe. As you get your fruity, creative groove going in the kitchen, feel free to mix up the flavors and find a new favorite. Start here, swirl anywhere.

Raspberry Variegate

Using pureed and whole fresh raspberries gives the variegate a wonderful texture. The whole berries will break down some, but they will still give you big bursts of raspberry in your gelato.

INGREDIENTS:

½ cup (6 oz. or 170g) raspberry puree or mashed fresh raspberries

¾ cup (3 oz. or 85g) fresh raspberries

⅞ cup (7 oz. or 200g) sugar

2 tablespoons (1 oz. or 28g) fresh lemon juice

1 teaspoon (5g) sea salt

Place all of the ingredients in a small saucepan. Over medium heat, stirring constantly, cook the raspberry mixture until it has thickened and reduced, about 10 minutes. Remove from heat and place in a covered container. Cool completely before incorporating. This makes a wonderful jam, topping for a dish of gelato or swirled into your favorite frozen flavor.

Yield: 14 oz.

WILD MAINE BLUEBERRY VARIEGATE

Here is the luscious ribbon of succulent wild blueberries that runs through the Maine Wild Blueberry Crisp gelato. The vanilla base, blueberry swirl, and oat crisp crunch are the perfect trio in one cup. Fresh or frozen berries both work well so you can make this all year long.

INGREDIENTS:

1½ cups (8 oz. or 226g) wild Maine blueberries

1 cup (8 oz. or 226g) white sugar

2 tablespoons (1 oz. or 28g) fresh lemon juice

1 teaspoon (5g) sea salt

Add the blueberries, sugar, lemon juice and salt to a 2-quart saucepan. Stir over medium heat until the mixture has reduced and thickened to the consistency of maple syrup, about 10 minutes. Remove from heat and transfer to a covered container. Cool completely before incorporating into frozen gelato. When cooled, the finished variegate will be the consistency of thick jam. In fact, it's also great on toast!

Yield: 17 oz.

Fig Fig Fig Variegate

Three little figgies— dried, jam, and fresh—make up this thick, sweet, vanilla- scented variegate. Also delicious on its own, with cheese, or swirled into mascarpone or caramel gelato.

INGREDIENTS:

About 8 (1 oz. or 28g) dried figs, chopped

½ cup (5 oz. or 142g) fig jam

¾ cup (8 oz. or 226g) Sugar Syrup (see below)

About 6 (3 oz. or 85g) fresh figs, stem removed and thinly sliced

1 vanilla bean

Prepare the vanilla bean: slice the vanilla bean in half lengthwise. Laying it flat on a cutting board, scrape the tiny seeds out with a paring knife and place them in a small dish. Set aside.

Place the dried figs, fig jam, sugar syrup, and sliced, empty vanilla bean pod in a small saucepan. Stirring constantly over medium-low heat, cook the mixture until it reduces and thickens; about 15 minutes. Remove the vanilla bean pod and discard.

Remove from the heat and stir in the fresh figs and vanilla bean seeds until thoroughly incorporated. Once the fig mixture is cool, place in a covered container. Chill completely before incorporating into any gelato. When cooled the finished variegate will be the consistency of thick jam.

Yield: 14 oz.

• •

Sugar Syrup

Lightly caramelized sugar syrup sweetens and adds body to our sorbettos, allowing them to freeze smoothly in the perfect sugar to water to fat ratio. The trick to the flavor is letting the syrup cook to a golden hue. With a candy thermometer, it's easy to stick to the numbers for a perfect batch every time. Sugar Syrup, stored in a covered jar or bottle, will keep for weeks in the refrigerator. You can even divide a batch into smaller jars and add a vanilla bean, citrus zest, fresh mint leaves, cinnamon sticks, hibiscus, or chai spices. The extra ingredients will steep in the sugar syrup and infuse their flavor. They're also great in tea, spritzers, and cocktails.

INGREDIENTS:

1½ cups (12 oz. or 340g) water

3½ cups (28 oz. or 794g) white granulated sugar

Place water into a 2-quart saucepan over medium heat. Stir in sugar and heat to 180 degrees on a candy thermometer. The mixture should be a light golden color. Remove from the heat, cool, and pour into an airtight container. Refrigerate until chilled. Sugar syrup will keep for a week or more in the refrigerator. Be sure it is completely cold before adding to your sorbetto recipe.

Yield: 1 qt.

❦INCLUSIONS❧

Several goodies we fold, stir, and mix into our gelato flavors are made in-house at Gelato Fiasco's Flavor Foundry in Brunswick, Maine. As you're choosing what chunky bits to include in your gelato, keep in mind that chilling the elements before incorporating into the recipe is one more way to make delicious gelato. The colder the inclusion, the less the churned gelato will melt; the less it melts, the fewer ice crystals; the fewer ice crystals, the smoother and more flavorful your gelato. Win!

OAT CRISP TOPPING

Our famous Maine Wild Blueberry Crisp among other delicious fruit crisps, incorporates the traditional crunchy topping right into the gelato. At the shop we pulse the oats in the food processor to make all the crisp pieces uniform and tiny, so you get the nugget of crunch without it being too hard or chewy. For your gelato at home, feel free to do the same or leave your oats whole for a bigger bite of crisp. Each gelato recipe uses about an ounce (approximately ⅓ cup) of the mixture. Save the rest to top your morning yogurt, a bowl of fresh fruit, your favorite fruit pie, or even warm homemade applesauce.

INGREDIENTS:

1½ cups (5¼ oz. or 150g) rolled oats (optional—pulse in food processor for a finer crumb)

½ cup (2 oz. or 57g) flour

1 cup, packed (8 oz. or 227g) brown sugar

2 sticks (1 cup or 8 oz. or 227g) unsalted butter

Preheat your oven to 375 degrees. In a medium bowl, mix the oats, flour, and brown sugar. Slice the butter into ½-inch pieces. Add the butter to the flour mixture. Using your fingers, gently work the butter into the dry ingredients until it resembles coarse crumbs. Spread the mixture in an even layer on a parchment-lined baking sheet. Bake at 375 degrees for about 20 minutes. Stir the crisp on the sheet pan and shake to distribute into a single layer. Bake for another 20 minutes, checking every five minutes, until the crisp is golden brown. Remove from the oven and cool completely. Store in a sealed container in the freezer.

Yield: 3 cups.

Nut Brittle

For mixing into gelato, topping, or snacking. Candy making is always a place to use caution and sometimes special equipment. A probe thermometer is especially useful when making smaller batches of brittle. A standard glass candy thermometer often needs a bit more depth to properly register the temperature correctly, but the probe can be held to instantly read in a shallow mixture.

INGREDIENTS:

1½ cups (12 oz. or 284g) white sugar

5 cups (20 oz. or 568g) toasted nuts, chopped

2½ teaspoons (10g) baking soda

2 teaspoons (10g) sea salt

½ cup (4 oz. or 113g) unsalted butter plus 1 tablespoon for greasing the pan

Another 1½ cups (12 oz. or 284g) white sugar

1¼ cups (15 oz. or 425g) honey

Preheat oven to 325 degrees and grease a sheet pan with 1 tablespoon butter or nonstick spray.

In a large bowl, mix together 1½ cups sugar, chopped nuts, baking soda and sea salt. Set aside.

In a heavy-bottomed saucepan, combine ½ cup butter, 1½ cups sugar and honey. Cook on high, stirring often, until mixture reaches 285 degrees.

As soon as the cooked sugar mixture comes up to temperature, remove from heat and pour the nut and sugar mixture into the pot. Stir until well combined.

Pour the still-hot mixture onto the greased baking sheet and spread evenly.

Immediately put the sheet pan into the preheated 325-degree oven and cook for about 20 minutes or until the sugars have caramelized. Remove the pan from the oven and allow the mixture cool at room temperature for an hour or until easy to handle.

Chop the brittle into pieces and enjoy! Store in an airtight container or sealable plastic bags in a dry area for up to a month. To keep longer, store in the freezer.

Yield: 6 cups.

MAPLE CINNAMON PECANS

These candied pecans are a lot like pieces of brittle. They are perfect added as an inclusion to your favorite gelato, or drizzled with a puddle of Dangerous Caramel, chilled and then dipped in melted chocolate. If you prefer walnuts, macadamia nuts, almonds, or hazelnuts, you can substitute them for pecans. Spring Break Maple and Honey in Smyrna Mills, Maine, has wonderful single origin Maine maple sugar available all year round along with their syrup and honey selections.

INGREDIENTS:

1 cup (5½ oz. or 156g) maple sugar

1 cup (8 oz. or 226g) white sugar

1½ cup (4 oz. or 113g) cold water

1 teaspoon (6g) sea salt

1 tablespoon (½ oz. of 14g) pure vanilla extract

1 teaspoon (7g) cinnamon

4 cups (46 oz. or 1304g) coarsely chopped pecans (or other nuts)

Line a cookie sheet with parchment paper. Place the sugars, water, and salt in a saucepan. Stir and bring to a boil. Cook until the mixture reaches 240 degrees on a candy thermometer (about 5 minutes).

Add the vanilla and cinnamon. Stir until blended. The mixture may bubble up and splatter, so be careful. Add the nuts. Stir to coat evenly, and immediately pour out onto the cookie sheet lined with parchment. Cool until easy to handle. If necessary, break nuts apart or coarsely chop before serving or adding to gelato. Be certain that the pecans are chilled before adding to gelato.

Yield: 64 oz.

CHOCOLATE CHIP COOKIE DOUGH

This is similar to your favorite cookies with one important omission. There are no eggs in this recipe, so no worries about eating the dough raw. Have at it! To use in gelato, chill the dough then roll into pinkie finger diameter ropes. Slice the ropes into dime-sized pieces and place in a single layer on a parchment lined baking sheet. Freeze. Once frozen, the pieces can be stored in a plastic zip-top bag or airtight container in the freezer. When you're ready to fold into a batch of gelato the dimes of dough will add a chewy, chocolatey burst of flavor.

INGREDIENTS:

1¼ cups (5½ oz. or 156g) all-purpose flour

½ teaspoon (3g) baking soda

½ teaspoon (3g) salt

½ cup (4 oz. or 113g) butter, softened

½ cup (4 oz. or 113g) granulated white sugar

½ cup (4 oz. or 113g) packed brown sugar

2 teaspoons (10g) vanilla extract

2 tablespoons (½ oz. or 14g) cornstarch mixed with 2 tablespoons (1 oz. or 28g) cold water

4 oz. (114g) chocolate fondant bar cut up into ¼-inch chips

You may wish toast the flour for several minutes to kill any potential bacteria. Combine flour, baking soda, and salt in small bowl. Cream butter, granulated sugar, brown sugar and vanilla in large mixer bowl. Add cornstarch mixture a little at a time, beating well after each addition; gradually beat in flour mixture. Stir in chips. Refrigerate until ready to use.

Yield: Enough for one batch of gelato.

BIG COUNTY BROWNIES

These moist and chewy Big County Brownies are great chopped up for your gelato, sliced into squares to make a brownie gelato sundae, or stacked with gelato in between and dipped in melted chocolate to make a decadent gelato sandwich. You will need a total of two cups of chocolate chips for this recipe—one to melt and another to fold into the batter just before baking. If you prefer milk or bittersweet chocolate chips, feel free to use what you love! To make Mint Big County Brownies, substitute mint chocolates, like Andes, After-Eight's, or Junior Mints in place of the chocolate chips.

INGREDIENTS:

1 cup (8 oz. or 226g) unsalted butter

¾ cup (4 oz. or 113g) unsweetened chocolate, chopped into chocolate chip sized pieces

1¼ cups (8 oz. or 226g) semisweet chocolate chips to melt

Plus another 1¼ cups (8 oz. or 226g) chocolate chips to fold into the batter

4 large eggs

1½ cups (12 oz. or 340g) white sugar

1 cup (4½ oz. or 120g) all purpose flour

⅓ cup (1 oz. or 28g) cocoa

½ teaspoon (2g) salt

Preheat oven to 350 degrees.

Melt butter, unsweetened chocolate and the 1 cup semisweet chocolate chips in a double boiler. Set aside until cool.

In a large bowl, beat eggs with sugar until thickened and the sugar has begun to dissolve. Add the melted butter/chocolate mixture. Stir until completely smooth. Add flour, cocoa and salt. Stir until incorporated and there are no lumps. Fold in the last ¼ cup of chocolate chips.

Line a greased 9- x 13-inch pan with parchment or foil and grease it well. Spread batter evenly into pan. Bake for 25 minutes or until the center of the pan is set. Cool. Run a sharp knife around the edges of the pan to release the brownies. Lift brownies out in one piece and cool completely (unless you can't resist- then have a little piece—it melts in your mouth when it is warm) Gently peel off paper or foil and cut to your desired shape.

If you'd like to bake them in tiny muffin tins, be sure to either use cupcake liners or spray or grease them very well. Bake for 12 to 15 minutes and check for done-ness.

If you are using the brownies in your gelato, chop them into ¼- to ½-inch chunks and place the pieces in a single layer on a sheet pan. Cover the pan and place in the freezer. Adding them cold is one secret to great Big County Brownie Gelato!

When they are completely cool, you can wrap them up and freeze for up to a week.

ROASTED MAPLE CANDIED BACON

Sweet, smoky, and salty, with a little spice. We're giving you a recipe for a pound of bacon. If you're a bacon lover, you can double it. For special occasions, we've been known to make up 10 pounds and give little bundles as gifts.

This candied bacon is roasted in the oven and, unlike cooking it in a pan, the bacon lays flat, which makes for easy chopping. If you're not a fan of maple, you can substitute molasses or honey for the syrup and brown or coconut sugar for the maple sugar. The liquid ingredients each make for a different flavor. The bourbon compliments the maple flavor. The port is sweet and more dessert-like. The rice vinegar gives the sweetness a delicate but punctuated counterpoint.

INGREDIENTS:

1 lb. (16 oz. or 454g) thick sliced bacon

1 tablespoon (14g) bourbon or port or unseasoned rice vinegar

3 tablespoons (2 oz. or 56g) pure Maine maple syrup

½ cup (2¾ oz. or 78g) maple sugar

½ cup (4 oz. or 113g) dark brown sugar

½ teaspoon (2g) freshly cracked black pepper

¼ teaspoon (1g) cayenne pepper (optional)

Preheat your oven to 350 degrees. Line two sheet pans with aluminum foil. The pans should have at least 1-inch sides to contain the rendered fat from the bacon. Set a metal cooling rack on each of the pans.

Next, set two pie plates or shallow bowls side by side with your baking pans handy. In one pie plate, add the liquids. Mix the bourbon or port or rice vinegar with the maple syrup. In the second pie plate, stir together the maple sugar, brown sugar, black pepper and cayenne (optional). Shake the dish slightly to make an even surface for the next step.

Dip each slice of bacon in the liquid then press each side into the sugar and pepper mixture. Carefully lay the slices on the cooling rack in the baking pan. If you handle the coated slices too much, the sugar may fall off. Try to leave ½ inch between the slices. They will shrink as they cook but you don't want them to stick together.

Roast the bacon in the preheated oven for 10 minutes. If your oven heats unevenly, you may want to rotate the pans 180 degrees every five minutes. Remove one pan at a time at 10 minutes and, with tongs, gently turn over each slice. Use caution, any fat on the bacon can drip on the hot foil and spatter. Sprinkle the turned slices with more of the remaining sugar from your coating step above. Return the pans to the oven and roast another 10 minutes or until the bacon is golden brown and cooked but not burned.

Line a large plate with parchment paper or foil. Remove the cooked bacon and set it to rest on the lined plate. Cool 20 minutes. Save the rendered bacon fat (on the baking pans or plate) in a jar in the refrigerator for future recipes.

Yield: 1 lb. cooked bacon.

WAFFLE CONES

Waffle cones make me think of Francesca—one of our first employees and currently our Employee Experience Officer. She started when she was in high school and kept coming back. She's about as close to a lifer as Bruno and I! When we first opened, she was the only person on the staff who could make waffle cones, and she would be drafted several times to make them during a shift just to keep up with demand.

Delicate and golden, they are like thin, crispy wafers. If you have a pizzelle iron, or a waffle iron with two-sided metal plates, you can cook this batter as you would pizzelles. In order to form a cup shape, you can turn ramekins upside down and lay the hot circles over them. The cone "cookies" are soft enough when they're hot to relax over the ramekins as they cool. Once cool they'll be crisp enough to use as a "bowl" for your gelato.

If you want a cone shape, you'll probably want to invest in a waffle cone maker. These are easily available online and at cooking supply stores. They usually don't cost too much and come with a specially shaped rolling tool to make the right shape for a waffle cone. We've made about a million waffle cones by now, so we have developed the knack for it, but with a bit of practice, you'll be rolling them in no time.

INGREDIENTS:

5⅛ cups (22 oz. or 681g) all-purpose flour

4⅛ cups (22 oz. or 681g) powdered sugar

1 tablespoon (7g) ground cinnamon

1 tablespoon (7g) freshly grated nutmeg
   (about one whole clove of nutmeg)

4 cups (32 oz. or 907g) heavy cream

2 tablespoons (28g) pure vanilla extract

Begin by preheating your waffle cone iron. Combine dry ingredients.

In a mixing bowl add vanilla extract to the heavy cream. Whip cream with a hand mixer until it reaches soft peaks. (The peaks should stand only for a split second when the beaters are removed.) Gently fold dry ingredients into the cream/vanilla mixture by hand. Continue until all of the dry ingredients are incorporated. Be careful not to over-mix. Cover and refrigerate for 30 minutes before using.

Place a golf ball-sized scoop of batter in the center of the preheated waffle cone iron. It doesn't take long (40 to 50 seconds) for the batter to cook and start turning a golden brown (keep in mind the underside of the waffle will be darker than the top side you see).

At that point, use a heat-safe spatula to remove the cooked waffle and lay it flat on a paper towel. Using a heat-safe cone roller, position the tip at a 10 o'clock position on waffle about 1 to 2 centimeters from the edge. Slowly roll the waffle cone from left to right, being sure to keep the cone tight around the base (if the base of the cone is even a little bit loose, the top will have far too much slack and lose its shape).

Once rolled, pinch the bottom point and lay the cone to rest along its seam. It only takes about 2 to 3 minutes to cool and retain its shape (just enough time to finish another cone or two).

BRUNO'S AND JOSH'S DREAM GELATO

JOSH: I'm an unabashed chunks guy. For me, the more the better. My dream gelato is a soft eating, chocolate fudge-esque swirl with chunks of dough batters and/or pieces of cake. I want the gelato to have some bitterness (think espresso) to play off the sweetness of the chunks. I love our Chocolate Raspberry Jam Gelato because it features the swirl of tart raspberry jam, which plays perfectly with the dark chocolate gelato and the dark chocolate fudge chunks. It's perfect.

BRUNO: In the way that most Chinese food is simply a vehicle for duck sauce, I find ice cream is just a platform for other stuff. Enough hot fudge, marshmallow, peanut butter, and caramel sauce can assist most weak flavored ice creams. When it comes to gelato, the flavor and silkiness are the boss. We have had a lot of great chunky flavors, but the smooth ones don't need all that fluff. The classics, such as Special Hazelnut and Peanut Butter Dream, are frequent players in my best dreams. I also think the Brownie Batter, Cake Batter, Tangerine, and Strawberry Balsamic do the trick as well. How can you go wrong when everything tastes so swell?

Toppings

❧DARK CHOCOLATE GANACHE❧

Make this topping to put on top of just about any gelato flavor for 100 bonus points. Add salty Spanish peanuts to that and add 500 bonus points.

INGREDIENTS:

1¼ cups (10 oz. or 284g) heavy cream

1 lightly packed cup (7 oz. or 190g) brown sugar

¼ cup (2 oz. or 57g) unsalted butter

3 cups (18 oz. or 510g) chocolate chips

1 teaspoon (2g) sea salt

1 tablespoon (½ oz. or 14g) pure vanilla extract

In a medium sauce pan, heat the cream just until it comes to a boil. Immediately add the brown sugar and stir until it has dissolved. Add the butter, salt, and vanilla; stirring until the butter has melted. Remove from the heat and add the chocolate chips. Whisk until fully incorporated, melted, and smooth.

Serve over your favorite gelato.

❧ CARAMEL SAUCES FOR TOPPINGS ❧

DANGEROUS SMOKED CARAMEL SAUCE

Sweet and smoky, this caramel sauce adds a special dimension to your gelato. Wearing snug, long sleeves or a chef's jacket will protect your arms—this caramel is not for the faint of heart. Only the bravest, most experienced need try this recipe. You'll need a candy thermometer and a measuring cup with a spout or small pitcher to pour the cream.

INGREDIENTS:

1¼ cups (9 oz. or 250g) white cane sugar

1¼ cups, firmly packed (9 oz. or 250g) dark brown sugar

1½ teaspoons (8g) sea salt

1¼ cups (10½ oz. or 300g) heavy cream

1 tablespoon (15g) pure vanilla extract, whiskey, rum, or brandy (optional)

In a small bowl, mix sugars and salt until thoroughly combined. Pour cream into a liquid measuring cup with a spout and handle, or a small pitcher.

Heat a large, heavy-bottomed pot on high. Divide the sugar mixture into thirds. Place one third of the mixed sugars into the pot. Move the sugars around a bit while they start melting. Constant mixing is not necessary until most of the sugars have melted and begun to smoke. Dissolve any crystals forming on the side of the pan with a wet pastry brush. Once the sugars in the pot have all melted, add about another third of the mixed sugars to the pot, now stirring constantly. As you stir, try to keep the melted sugar away from the sides of the pot. Once they have melted, repeat the last step with the remaining third of the sugars.

Once _all_ of the sugars have melted, place the thermometer into the melted sugar mixture. You are shooting for anywhere between 300 and 345 degrees, depending on the flavor you want the caramel to have. Lighter, sweeter flavors result from the cooler temperature, and darker, deeper caramelization results from the higher.

At the desired temperature turn off the heat and immediately start adding cream, very slowly, while stirring constantly. BE CAREFUL of steam and bubbling sugar in this step. Steam gets very hot and the violent bubbling can spatter quite a long distance—here's where the long sleeves come in handy.

Once all cream has been added, flavor the caramel with whatever you like. Try 1 tablespoon whiskey, rum, brandy or pure vanilla extract. Once the flavor has been incorporated, remove from the heat and cool to room temperature before serving.

Smooth Caramel Sauce

This caramel sauce is rich, supple, and buttery. Add a sprinkle of coarse sea salt over the top for a lasting salty crunch.

INGREDIENTS:

2¼ cups (16 oz. or 454g) white sugar

½ cup (4 oz. or 118ml) water

1 tablespoon (15ml) lemon juice

2 teaspoons (12g) sea salt

10 tablespoons (6 oz. or 142g) unsalted butter

1 cup (8½ oz. or 241g) heavy cream

Place sugar, water, lemon juice, and salt into a heavy-bottomed, medium saucepan over medium low heat and stir until sugar has dissolved. Dissolve any crystals forming on the side of the pan with a wet pastry brush.

Once sugar has dissolved, increase heat to high. At this point, do not stir the mixture directly. Now and then, holding the handle of the pan, give the pot a swirl to keep the mixture moving. The mixture will start to bubble after a minute or so. After 3 to 4 minutes the mixture will turn from a light amber to medium amber. Medium amber is the color you want for this sauce.

Turn the heat down to medium and whisk in the butter, one tablespoon at a time, being careful as the mixture will bubble wildly. Remove from heat and whisk the heavy cream into the caramel until it is smooth and uniform in color.

Allow the caramel to cool for 20 minutes before serving. Serve over your favorite gelato. Store remaining caramel in a covered container in the refrigerator for up to a week.

Yield: About 2 lbs.

Gelato

❦ ALLEN'S COFFEE BRANDY ❦

Often called the "Champagne of Maine," Allen's Coffee Brandy is a rich espresso-hued liqueur that has been a favorite cocktail flavor for generations.

INGREDIENTS:

4 cups (32 oz. or 907g) Classic White Gelato Base or Yellow Gelato Base

⅓ cup (4 oz. or 113g) Allen's Coffee Brandy

½ cup (4 oz. or 113g) black coffee or espresso

Place the coffee brandy and black coffee into a small saucepan. Cook over medium heat until the mixture has reduced by a third to 6 ounces, about 15 minutes. Cool.

In a large bowl whisk together the Gelato Base and coffee reduction until mixture is smooth. Place in a covered container and refrigerate until cold, 4 hours or overnight.

Once the base has chilled, churn it in your home ice cream maker.

Yield: 40 oz. (about 3 pints).

Our Store Hours

Ever since our first month, we've attempted to keep regular, easy-to-remember hours that do not change season-to-season. The thought was that if we changed the hours whenever the seasons changed, people would begin to doubt if we were open, so they wouldn't risk adventuring to find us closed on a Maine October night. So, we vowed to keep the same hours year round. Also, the hours are minimum hours. We do not turn people away at the door no matter what time of day they come.

If we are inside the store and you show up after our official close time, please just give us a knock. Someone will take off their jacket and give you a dish of gelato to take home.

❦ APPLE MASCARPONE ❧

Mascarpone cheese makes this fall flavor profoundly creamy. A caramel swirl or pecans can be added for additional taste and texture.

INGREDIENTS:

3 cups (24 oz. or 680g) Classic White Gelato Base

8-oz. tub (226g) mascarpone cheese

⅓ cup (3 oz. or 85g) brown sugar

1½ cups (12 oz. or 340g) no sugar added applesauce

In a large bowl, whisk together the warm Gelato Base, mascarpone cheese and brown sugar until cheese has melted and the mixture is smooth. Add the applesauce and whisk thoroughly. Place in a covered container and refrigerate until cold, 4 hours or overnight.

Once the base has chilled, churn it in your home ice cream maker.

Yield: 46 oz. (about 3 pints).

APPLE PIE A LA MODE

With a delightful blend of spices, this recipe seeks to replicate apple pie filling as a gelato flavor. Use applesauce from a Maine orchard for best results.

INGREDIENTS:

3 cups (24 oz. or 680g) Classic White Gelato Base

1 cup (8 oz. or 226g) applesauce

¼ cup (2 oz. or 56g) brown sugar

¼ teaspoon (2g) ground allspice

¼ teaspoon (2g) ground cloves

¼ teaspoon (2g) ground ginger

2 teaspoon (5g) cinnamon

In a large bowl whisk together the Classic White Gelato Base, applesauce, brown sugar, allspice, cloves, ginger and cinnamon until mixture is smooth and uniform in color. Place in a covered container and refrigerate until cold, 4 hours or overnight.

Once the gelato has chilled, churn it in your home ice cream maker.

Yield: 34 oz. (about 2 pints).

⸘BIG COUNTY BROWNIE⸘

Brownie batter chunks forge chocolate flavor as big as Maine's largest county is wide. Aroostook County is the crown of Maine. Known just as "The County" or "God's Country," time seems to slow, the further north you travel. At the crest of each rolling hill, it's as if a patchwork quilt was thrown out to cover the acres stitching the fields together with mossy stone walls. Folks in the County know how to enjoy life, savoring each moment, the way life should be. This big, chocolatey, brownie-studded gelato is our ode to Aroostook.

INGREDIENTS:

- 4 cups (32 oz. or 907g) Decadent Chocolate Gelato Base
- ⅓ cup (1.5 oz. or 43g) cake flour
- ¼ cup (¾ oz. or 21g) cocoa powder
- ½ cup (2⅔ oz. or 75g) powdered sugar
- ⅓ cup (2 oz. or 56g) semisweet chocolate chunks
- 4 oz. (113g) chopped brownies (one 4- x 4-inch brownie)

You may wish to toast the cake flour for several minutes to kill any bacteria. In a large bowl, whisk together the Gelato Base, cake flour, cocoa, and powdered sugar until the mixture is smooth and uniform in color.

Place in a covered container and refrigerate until cold, 4 hours or overnight. Place the chocolate chunks and chopped brownies in a covered container along with a 2-quart metal bowl in the freezer.

Once the gelato has chilled, churn it in your home ice cream maker. When the gelato is done freezing, scoop it into the cold bowl. Add the cold chocolate chunks and brownie pieces and fold together so the pieces are evenly distributed. Once combined, put lid on stainless steel bowl and put in freezer until ready to be eaten.

Yield: 42 oz. (about 3 pints).

⋑ BISCUIT BATTER WITH RASPBERRY JAM ⋐

Good raspberry jam takes a fresh biscuit to the next level. This recipe creates a biscuit batter gelato and adds a generous swirl of fresh raspberry jam.

INGREDIENTS:

4 cups (32 oz. or 907g) Classic White Gelato Base

½ cup (2 oz. or 57g) cake flour

¼ cup (1¼ oz. or 35g) Carnation malted milk powder

1 cup (5⅓ oz. or 150g) powdered sugar

2 teaspoons (10g) pure vanilla extract

½ cup (6 oz. or 170g) Cold Raspberry Variegate

You may wish to toast the cake flour for several minutes to kill any bacteria. In a large bowl, whisk together the Classic White Gelato Base, cake flour, malted milk powder, powdered sugar, and vanilla until mixture is smooth and uniform in color. Place in a covered container and refrigerate until cold, 4 hours or overnight.

Once the gelato has chilled, churn it in your home ice cream maker. When the gelato is finished churning, fold in the cold raspberry swirl so there are ribbons of fruit throughout the gelato but it is not completely incorporated. Once combined, replace lid on stainless steel bowl and return it to the freezer.

Yield: 54 oz. (about 4 pints).

⋑ BLACK AND PINK PEPPERCORN ⋐

Not for the faint of heart! Peppercorns bring a hefty dose of the unexpected to fresh cream gelato. We find that a minority of our customers like spicy flavors—but those who do, love the heat!

INGREDIENTS:

4 cups (32 oz. or 907g) Classic White Gelato Base

1½ teaspoons (2g) crushed or coarsely ground black peppercorns

1 teaspoon (2g) crushed or coarsely ground pink peppercorns

In a large bowl whisk together the Classic White Gelato Base, black and pink peppercorns until mixture is smooth and the peppercorns are evenly distributed. Place in a covered container and refrigerate until cold, 4 hours or overnight.

Once the gelato has chilled, churn it in your home ice cream maker.

Yield: 32 oz. (about 2 pints).

BLACK TEA/ EARL GREY TEA

Slightly sweet with hints of bergamot, all it needs is a crumpet.

INGREDIENTS:

3 cups (24 oz. or 680g) Classic White Gelato Base

1 cup (8 oz. or 227g) cooled, strongly brewed tea—3 teabags in 8 oz. of water

2 tablespoons (1 oz. or 28g) sugar

½ cup (1 oz. or 28g) skim milk powder

In a large bowl whisk together the Classic White Gelato Base, tea, sugar and skim milk powder until mixture is smooth and uniform in color. Place in a covered container and refrigerate until cold, 4 hours or overnight.

Once the gelato has chilled, churn it in your home ice cream maker.

Yield: 33 oz. (about 2 pints).

• •

BLUEBERRY PIE

It doesn't get much better than a creamy blueberry gelato with extra pieces of blueberry pie!

INGREDIENTS:

4 cups (32 oz. or 907g) Classic White Gelato Base

½ cup (4 oz. or 113g) fresh Maine wild blueberries

¼ cup (1⅓ oz. or 37g) powdered sugar

6 oz. (170g) chopped blueberry pie—approximately ⅛ piece of whole pie, cut into ½-inch chunks

In a large bowl, whisk together the Classic White Gelato Base, blueberries, and powdered sugar until mixture is smooth and uniform in color. Place in a covered container and refrigerate until cold, 4 hours or overnight. Place the chopped blueberry pie in a covered container in the freezer. Chill a 2-quart metal bowl in the freezer.

Once the gelato has chilled, churn it in your home ice cream maker according to the manufacturer's instructions. When the gelato is done freezing, scoop gelato into the cold bowl. Add the cold blueberry pie pieces and fold together gently so the pieces are evenly distributed. Don't over mix. Once combined put lid on the stainless steel bowl and put in freezer until you're ready to eat.

Yield: 43 oz. (about 3 pints).

❧ BOSTON CREAM PIE ❧

Paul Revere would ride here for this one. Fragrant, rich, vanilla gelato, akin to Bavarian Cream, is dotted with pound cake and chunks of chocolate, giving each bite a taste the Parker House would be proud of.

INGREDIENTS:

4 cups (32 oz. or 907g) Rich Yellow Gelato Base

4 teaspoons (20g) pure vanilla extract

1 cup (4 oz. or 113g) pound cake—chopped into ½-inch pieces

¼ cup (2 oz. or 57g) Sugar Syrup

½ cup (3 oz. or 85g) chocolate chunks

In a large bowl whisk together the Rich Yellow Gelato Base and vanilla until mixture is smooth and uniform in color. Place in a covered container and refrigerate until cold, 4 hours or overnight. Place the pound cake pieces in a zip top plastic bag. Drizzle sugar syrup over the cake and, with the bag closed, shake the bag gently to coat the pieces. Open a corner of the bag and remove most of the air. Place the bag along with the chocolate chunks in a 2-quart bowl. Cover and chill in the freezer.

Once the gelato has chilled, churn it in your home ice cream maker. When the gelato is done churning, scoop it into the cold bowl. Add the cold syrup coated cake pieces and chocolate and fold together so the pieces are evenly distributed. Once combined put lid on stainless steel bowl and return to freezer.

Yield: 41 oz. (about 3 pints).

ℰ BOURBON VANILLA ℱ

INGREDIENTS:

4 cups (32 oz. or 907g) Classic White Gelato Base

2 teaspoons (10g) pure vanilla extract

¼ cup (3 oz. or 85g) chilled bourbon reduction (see recipe below)

BOURBON REDUCTION

INGREDIENTS:

6 oz. bourbon

Pour the bourbon into a small heavy bottomed pan. Over medium heat, bring the bourbon up to a simmer and allow the liquid to reduce by half. Remove from heat and chill.

In a large bowl whisk together the Classic White Gelato Base, vanilla, and bourbon reduction until mixture is smooth and uniform in color. Place in a covered container and refrigerate until cold, 4 hours or overnight.

Once the gelato has chilled, churn it in your home ice cream maker.

Yield: 35 oz. (about 3 pints).

THE LEGENDARY TOAST

The first winter we were open was brutal and we needed more sales. We figured we had all of the equipment to make and serve coffee and might attract some coffee sales if we established ourselves as a coffee shop in the morning hours. But what to serve with the coffee? TOAST! We found a friend who could make delicious homemade bread and we served it with your choice of peanut butter, butter, or cinnamon and sugar. It didn't do much to attract the morning sales we were hoping for, but we did sell a lot of toast to people coming in at night. When our bread supplier quit the bread business, our artisanal toast aspirations died too.

To this day, there are customers who 1.) Ask us to bring back the toast! and 2.) Swear it was the best toast they ever had in their lives.

❀ CAKE BATTER ❀

We serve this flavor with rainbow sprinkles, because every day should be a celebration! Cake Batter Gelato was in the case the day the doors to Gelato Fiasco first opened. It's been a hit, and not just because we're always happy to shake on some extra sprinkles from the secret sprinkle shaker we keep behind the counter.

INGREDIENTS:

4 cups (32 oz. or 907g) Classic White Gelato Base

½ cup (2¼ oz. or 64g) cake flour

1 cup (5⅓ oz. or 150g) powdered sugar

2 teaspoons (10g) pure vanilla extract

You may wish to toast the cake flour for several minutes to kill any bacteria. In a large bowl whisk together the Classic White Gelato Base, cake flour, powdered sugar, and vanilla until mixture is smooth and uniform in color. Place in a covered container and refrigerate until cold, 4 hours or overnight.

Once the gelato has chilled, churn it in your home ice cream maker.

Yield: 39 oz. (about 3 pints).

❧ CANDIED GINGER ❧

INGREDIENTS:

4 cups (32 oz. or 907g) Classic White Gelato Base

¼ cup (1½ oz. or 42g) fresh ginger root, peeled and grated on a microplane or ginger grater

1 teaspoon (2g) ground ginger

⅔ cup (5 oz. or 142g) chopped candied ginger

In a large bowl whisk together the Classic White Gelato Base, grated fresh ginger, and ground ginger until the mixture is smooth and uniform in color. Place in a covered container and refrigerate until cold, 4 hours or overnight. Place the chopped candied ginger in a zip top plastic bag, along with a 2-quart metal bowl, in the freezer.

Once the gelato has chilled, churn it in your home ice cream maker. When the gelato is done freezing scoop gelato into the cold bowl. Add the cold chopped candied ginger and fold together gently so the pieces are evenly distributed. Once combined put lid on stainless steel bowl and return it to the freezer.

Yield: 38 oz. (about 3 pints).

• •

❧ CAPPUCCINO NUTMEG ❧

INGREDIENTS:

5 cups (40 oz. or 1134g) Classic White Gelato Base

1¼ cups (4 oz. or 113g) ground coffee

2 teaspoons (4g) ground nutmeg

In a large bowl whisk together the Classic White Gelato Base and ground coffee. Place the mixture in the refrigerator to steep for 2 hours. Strain the mixture and discard solids. Add nutmeg, stirring until mixture is smooth and uniform in color. Place in a covered container and refrigerate until cold, 2 more hours or overnight.

Once the gelato has chilled, churn it in your home ice cream maker.

Yield: 44 oz. (about 3 pints).

ᒥ CARAMEL BROWNIE ᒧ
PEANUT BUTTER CUP

INGREDIENTS:

4 cups (32 oz. or 907g) Classic White Gelato Base, chilled

¼ cup (3 oz. or 85g) Caramel Sea Salt Caramel

1 teaspoon (6g) sea salt

⅓ cup (2 oz. or 57g) chocolate chunks

½ cup (4 oz. or 113g) peanut butter cups- either miniature or larger chopped into ½-inch pieces

4 oz. (113g) chopped brownies (one 4- x 4-inch brownie)

(Optional: 10 naked chocolate kisses, unwrapped and chilled)

In a large bowl whisk together the Classic White Gelato Base, caramel sea salt caramel, and sea salt until mixture is smooth and uniform in color. Place in a covered container and refrigerate until cold, 4 hours or overnight. Place the chocolate chunks, peanut butter cups and chopped brownies (kisses too if you like) in a covered container in the freezer. Chill a 2-quart metal bowl in the freezer.

Once the gelato has chilled, churn it in your home ice cream maker. When the gelato is done freezing scoop it into the cold bowl. Add the cold chocolate chunks, peanut butter cups, and brownie pieces (and optional kisses) and fold together so the pieces are evenly distributed. Once combined put lid on stainless steel bowl and return it to the freezer.

Yield: 45 oz. (3 pints).

• •

ᒥ CARAMEL LATTE ᒧ

INGREDIENTS:

5 cups (40 oz. or 1134g) Classic White Gelato Base

1¼ cups (4 oz. or 113g) ground coffee

¼ cup (3 oz. or 85g) Smooth Caramel

In a large bowl whisk together the Gelato Base, and coffee. Place the mixture in the refrigerator to steep for 2 hours. Strain, discard coffee grounds. Add Smooth Caramel to the base, stirring until mixture is smooth and uniform in color. Place in a covered container and refrigerate until cold, 4 hours or overnight.

Once the gelato has chilled, churn it in your home ice cream maker.

Yield: 47 oz. (3+ pints).

❦ CARAMEL SEA SALT ❧

Several years ago, we observed that Caramel Sea Salt Gelato would sell out in our shops every time we offered it. Always knowing a good thing when we see (or taste) one, we decided to start offering it daily, and it became one of our greatest break-out-hit flavors of all time. It's salty. Bruno has always believed that if an ingredient deserved to be in a flavor's name, it had to assert itself in the actual flavor.

INGREDIENTS:

4 cups (32 oz. or 907g) Classic White Gelato Base

¼ cup (3 oz. or 85g) Caramel Sea Salt Caramel

½ teaspoon (3g) coarse sea salt

In a large bowl whisk together the warm Classic White Gelato Base and Caramel Sea Salt Caramel until mixture is smooth and uniform in color. Place in a covered container and refrigerate until cold, 4 hours or overnight.

Once the gelato has chilled, churn it in your home ice cream maker. When the gelato has finished churning, fold in the sea salt until it is evenly distributed. Once combined put lid on stainless steel bowl and return it to the freezer.

Yield: 35 oz. (about 3 pints).

﴾CARAMELIZED BANANA﴿

INGREDIENTS:

3 cups (24 oz. or 680g) Classic White Gelato Base

1¼ cups (8 oz. or 227g) mashed ripe banana

⅛ cup (1 oz. or 28g) packed brown sugar

¾ cup (6 oz. or 170g) Cold Banana Caramel

Using a food processor, blender or immersion blender puree the Classic White Gelato Base, mashed banana, and brown sugar until mixture is smooth and uniform in color. Place in a covered container and refrigerate until cold, 4 hours or overnight. Chill a 2-quart metal bowl in the freezer.

Once the gelato has chilled, churn it in your home ice cream maker. When the gelato is done freezing scoop gelato into the cold bowl. Add the Cold Banana Caramel and fold together until it is evenly distributed. Once combined put lid on stainless steel bowl and return it to the freezer.

Yield: 39 oz. (about 3 pints).

❧ CHAI ☙

Black tea and spices.

INGREDIENTS:

3 cups (24 oz. or 680g) Classic White Gelato Base

⅞ cup (7 oz. or 198g) Chai concentrate (found in the tea aisle of your supermarket)

½ cup (1 oz. or 28g) skim milk powder

¼ teaspoon (1g) ground allspice

In a large bowl whisk together the Classic White Gelato Base, chai concentrate, skim milk powder and ground allspice until mixture is smooth and uniform in color. Place in a covered container and refrigerate until cold, 4 hours or overnight.

Once the gelato has chilled, churn it in your home ice cream maker.

Yield: 32 oz. (about 2 pints).

• •

❧ CHEESECAKE ☙

INGREDIENTS:

3 cups (24 oz. or 680g) Classic White Gelato Base

1¼ cups (10 oz. or 283g) skim milk

¾ cup (6 oz. or 170g) cream cheese

½ cup (6 oz. or 170g) sugar syrup

1 teaspoon (5g) pure vanilla extract

½ teaspoon (3g) sea salt

In a large bowl whisk together the warm Classic White Gelato Base, skim milk, cream cheese, sugar syrup, vanilla and sea salt until cream cheese is melted and mixture is smooth and uniform in color. Place in a covered container and refrigerate until cold, 4 hours or overnight.

Once the gelato has chilled, churn it in your home ice cream maker.

Yield: 46 oz. (about 3+ pints).

₰CHOCOLATE BACON₰

INGREDIENTS:

4 cups (32 oz. or 907g) Decadent Chocolate
   Gelato Base

1 tablespoon (½ oz. or 14g) liquid smoke

1 tablespoon (½ oz. or 14g) pure vanilla
   extract

1 cup (4 oz. or 113g) chopped Roasted Maple
   Candied Bacon, ½-inch pieces

In a large bowl whisk together the Decadent
Chocolate Gelato Base, liquid smoke and
vanilla until mixture is smooth and uniform
in color. Place in a covered container and
refrigerate until cold, 4 hours or overnight.

Place the chopped candied bacon in covered
container along with a 2-quart metal bowl
in the freezer.

Once the gelato has chilled, churn it
in your home ice cream maker. When the
gelato is done freezing scoop into the cold
bowl. Add the cold candied bacon and
fold together so the pieces are evenly distributed. Once combined put lid on stainless steel bowl and return it to the freezer.

Yield: 36 oz (about 2 pints).

{CHOCOLATE BOURBON}

INGREDIENTS:

3 cups (24 oz. or 680g) Decadent Chocolate Gelato Base

1 cup (8 oz. or 227g) Classic White Gelato Base

¾ cup (6 oz. or 170g) bourbon

1 vanilla bean

1 tablespoon (½ oz. or 14g) pure vanilla extract

First make a vanilla bourbon reduction. On a cutting board or flat surface, cut the vanilla bean lengthwise. Using a small spoon or knife, scrape the vanilla bean seeds out of the pod and place them in a small covered dish. The seeds are sometimes called vanilla caviar. This amount will vary by the type, length and age of your vanilla bean. Cut the vanilla bean pod into four smaller pieces. Place the now seedless pod pieces in a small saucepan and add the bourbon. Over medium heat, bring the bourbon up to a simmer and allow the liquid to reduce by approximately 30%, so you're left with 4 ounces of reduction. Pour the reduction into a small container, cover, and chill.

In a large bowl whisk together the Decadent Chocolate Gelato Base, and Classic White Gelato Base. Remove the vanilla bean pod segments from the cold bourbon reduction. Reserve the pod in a sealed plastic bag in the freezer to use for other recipes or discard the remaining pod pieces. Whisk the reduction, vanilla bean seeds (vanilla caviar) and vanilla extract into the gelato bases until mixture is smooth and uniform in color. Make sure the vanilla bean seeds are distributed throughout and not clumped together. Place in a covered container and refrigerate until cold, 4 hours or overnight.

Once the gelato has chilled, churn it in your home ice cream maker.

Yield: 38 oz. (about 3 pints).

NICE PEOPLE

Desserts should be fun to create, fun to serve, and fun to enjoy. We hire kind and caring people, and try to support them in ways that help them create amazing desserts and experiences for our customers.

❧CHOCOLATE PEANUT BUTTER CUP❧

INGREDIENTS:

4 cups (32 oz. or 907g) Decadent Chocolate Gelato Base, chilled

1 cup (6 oz. or 170g) chopped peanut butter cups

Place the chopped peanut butter cups in a covered container along with a 2-quart metal bowl in the freezer.

Churn the Rich Chocolate Base in your home ice cream maker. When the gelato is done freezing scoop into the cold bowl. Add the cold peanut butter cups and fold together so the pieces are evenly distributed. Once combined put lid on stainless steel bowl and return it to the freezer.

Yield: 38 oz. (about 2 pints).

❧ CHURCH SUPPER GRAPE-NUT ❧

Full o' praise! In our neck of the woods, New England church suppers often ended with one of the dear church ladies' Grape-nut pudding. A rich, creamy custard dotted with soft and crunchy Grape-Nuts cereal tastes much like bread pudding minus the cinnamon. If you were lucky, it was served with a dollop of vanilla scented whipped cream or a scoop of ice cream. We've combined them all to make a luscious, vanilla, takes-me-back tasting gelato. Amen!

INGREDIENTS:

4 cups (32 oz. or 907g) Classic White Gelato Base

1 cup (5 oz. or 142g) Grape-Nuts cereal, separated into ⅔ and ⅓ amounts

1 tablespoon (14g) pure vanilla extract

In a large bowl whisk together the Classic White Gelato Base, ⅔ of the Grape-Nuts cereal, and vanilla until the cereal is incorporated evenly throughout. Place in a covered container and refrigerate until cold, 4 hours or overnight. Place the remaining ⅓ of the Grape-Nuts in a zip-top plastic bag and put it and a 2-quart metal bowl in the freezer to chill.

Once the gelato has chilled, churn it in your home ice cream maker. Once the gelato is done freezing scoop gelato into cold bowl. Add the cold Grape-Nuts and fold together. Once combined put lid on stainless steel bowl and return it to the freezer.

Yield: 37 oz. (about 3 pints).

MADE THE MAINE WAY

We are artisans and servers who care about our work and keep on tinkering, testing, and building until we get things right—then we try to make them still better. We are about our craft and back it up unconditionally with The Gelato Fiasco Guarantee.

❧ CINNAMON ❧

INGREDIENTS:

4 cups (32 oz. or 907g) Classic White Gelato Base

2 teaspoons (6g) Vietnamese or Saigon cinnamon

In a large bowl whisk together the Classic White Gelato Base and cinnamon until mixture is smooth and uniform in color. Place in a covered container and refrigerate until cold, 4 hours or overnight.

Once the gelato has chilled, churn it in your home ice cream maker.

Yield: 32 oz. (about 3 pints).

❧ COFFEE AND DOUGHNUTS ❧

Definitely a crowd-pleaser. We swear by Holy Donut in Portland, Maine, and Frosty's Donuts in Brunswick, Maine. You can use doughnuts from your favorite local shop; remember that the quality of the donuts will dramatically impact the final product. NOTE: This is a great flavor to pint as gifts for friends or family.

INGREDIENTS:

5 cups (40 oz. or 1134g) Classic White Gelato Base

1¼ cups (4 oz. or 113g) ground coffee

5 oz. (142g) doughnuts, chopped into ½-inch chunks (local homemade doughnut holes were two pieces per ounce so we used 10)

3 tablespoons (2 oz. or 57g) Sugar Syrup

Blend together the Gelato Base and coffee. Steep mixture in the refrigerator for 2 hours. Strain the coffee gelato base through a fine mesh sieve. Discard coffee grounds. Place the gelato in a covered container and refrigerate until cold, 4 hours or overnight. Put the chopped doughnuts into a zip top plastic bag. Pour in the Sugar Syrup and gently shake the bag until the pieces of doughnut are coated. Close the zip top bag, pressing out as much air as you can. Place it and a 2-quart metal bowl in the freezer to chill.

Once the gelato has chilled, churn it in your home ice cream maker. When the gelato is done freezing scoop it into the cold bowl. Add the sugar syrup coated doughnut pieces and fold together. Once combined put lid on stainless steel bowl and return it to the freezer.

Yield: 49 oz. (about 3+ pints).

⸲ COOKIE DOUGH ⸳

INGREDIENTS:

4 cups (32 oz. or 907g) Classic White Gelato Base, chilled

2 teaspoons (10g) pure vanilla extract

1¼ cup (8 oz. or 227g) Chocolate Chip Cookie Dough broken into dime-sized pieces

In a large bowl whisk together the Classic White Gelato Base, and vanilla until mixture is smooth and uniform in color. Place in a covered container and refrigerate until cold, 2 hours or overnight.

Prepare the cookie dough. Cover and chill the dough for 30 minutes, then roll into pinkie finger diameter ropes. Slice the ropes into dime sized pieces and place in a single layer on a parchment lined baking sheet. Freeze for 1 hour. Once frozen, the pieces can be stored in a plastic zip top bag or airtight container in the freezer. Close the zip top bag, pressing out as much air as you can. Place it and a 2-quart metal bowl in the freezer to chill.

Once the gelato has chilled, churn it in your home ice cream maker. When the gelato is done freezing scoop it into the cold bowl. Measure 1¼ cups (8 oz.) of cookie dough and fold it into the frozen gelato until evenly distributed throughout. Once combined cover the bowl and return it to the freezer.

Yield: 40 oz. (about 2 pints).

COOKIE THERAPY

There's nothing like cookies for comfort, especially when they're crushed crème-filled ones blended into cold, frothy milk. As we developed the recipe, we aimed for the ideal balance of creaminess, chocolate crispiness, and nostalgia. Generations agree: nothing goes better with Maine milk than all-natural chocolate cookies. This one will never go out of style. Nor should it.

INGREDIENTS:

4 cups (32 oz. or 907g) Classic White Gelato Base, chilled

2 teaspoons (10g) pure vanilla extract

¾ cup (4 oz. or 227g) chocolate cookie sandwiches broken into dime sized pieces

In a large bowl whisk together the Classic White Gelato Base, and vanilla until mixture is smooth and uniform in color. Place in a covered container and refrigerate until cold, 2 hours or overnight. Place the chocolate cookie sandwich pieces in a plastic zip top bag or airtight container in the freezer. Close the zip top bag, pressing out as much air as you can. Place it and a 2-quart metal bowl in the freezer to chill.

Once the base has chilled, churn it in your home ice cream maker. When the gelato is done freezing scoop it into the cold bowl. Fold the cold chocolate cookie pieces into the frozen gelato until evenly distributed. Once combined cover the bowl and return it to the freezer.

Yield: 36 oz. (about 2 pints).

❦ CREME ANGLAISE ❦

Like pastry chefs around the world, we believe that Creme Anglaise—which is simply a soft custard made from vanilla, sugar, egg yolks, and milk—improves anything it touches. It is worth taking the time to master this classic and then serve it with fresh berries, chocolate sauce, or in the middle of an ice cream sandwich.

INGREDIENTS:

4 cups (32 oz. or 907g) Rich Yellow Gelato Base, chilled

1 tablespoon (14g) pure vanilla extract

In a large bowl whisk together the Rich Yellow Gelato Base and vanilla until mixture is smooth and uniform in color. Place in a covered container and refrigerate until cold, 4 hours or overnight.

Once the base has chilled, churn it in your home ice cream maker.

Yield: 32 oz. (about 3 pints)

DARK CHOCOLATE CARAMEL SEA SALT

This is among the best-sellers for Gelato Fiasco in grocery stores: Rich, dark chocolate with sea-swept caramel. A decadent treat. Buttery. Classic. Salty-sweet.

INGREDIENTS:

4 cups (32 oz. or 907g) Decadent Chocolate Gelato Base

¼ cup (3 oz. or 85g) Caramel for Dark Chocolate Caramel Sea Salt Gelato

1½ teaspoons (8g) coarse sea salt

In a large bowl whisk together the warm Decadent Chocolate Gelato Base, and caramel until mixture is smooth and uniform in color. Place in a covered container and refrigerate until cold, 4 hours or overnight.

Once the base has chilled, churn it in your home ice cream maker. When the gelato has finished churning, fold in the sea salt until it is evenly distributed. Once combined put lid on stainless steel bowl and put in freezer.

Yield: 35 oz. (about 3 pints)

⧼ESPRESSO CHIP⧽

This flavor combines smooth, strong Sumatran coffee beans with spangled dark chocolate slivers. It's a coffee lover's delight. It's the most memorable coffee-and-chocolate dessert you'll ever try. Guaranteed.

INGREDIENTS:

4 cups (32 oz. or 907g) Classic White Gelato Base

1 cup (3 oz. or 85g) ground coffee (we love Sumatra roast from Wicked Joe Organic Coffee Co. in Maine, but choose your favorite beans)

½ cup (3 oz. or 85g) semi sweet chocolate chips

⅓ cup (1 oz. or 28g) bittersweet chocolate chips

Stir the coffee into the warm gelato base. Place in a covered container. Allow it to steep as it cools in the refrigerator for two hours. Strain the mixture through a fine mesh sieve and return it to the refrigerator. Discard the solids/coffee grounds. Continue to chill until cold, another 2 hours or overnight.

Once the base has chilled, churn it in your home ice cream maker.

While the gelato is churning, in a double boiler set over simmering water, melt the semi-sweet and bitter-sweet chocolate bits together. Allow chocolate to cool to room temperature, while it still remains fluid. If you prefer using only semi sweet or bittersweet, feel free to use 4 ounces of either.

When the gelato is has finished churning, Drizzle the cooled, fluid, melted chocolate over the frozen gelato and as it firms, using two spoons, break the pieces of chocolate up into small chunks. Stir the chocolate chunks into the finished gelato.

Yield: 36 oz. (about 3 pints)

❧ FALL IN BOURBON COUNTRY ❧

This pumpkin gelato is elevated by a shot of Wild Turkey bourbon, a twist of cinnamon-glazed pecans or nut brittle, and a swirl of buttery caramel.

INGREDIENTS:

3 cups (24 oz. or 680g) Classic White Gelato Base

1 cup (8 oz. or 227g) canned pumpkin, preferably One Pie

⅛ cup (2 oz. or 57g) molasses

¼ cup (2 oz. or 57g) Wild Turkey bourbon

1 teaspoon (2g) ground ginger

1½ teaspoons (3g) ground cinnamon

1 teaspoon (2g) ground nutmeg

¼ teaspoons (⅔g) ground cloves

¼ teaspoons (⅔g) ground allspice

¾ cup (4 oz. or 113g) chopped Maple Cinnamon Pecans or Nut Brittle

¼ cup (2 oz. or 57g) Smooth Caramel Sauce

In a large bowl whisk together the Classic White Gelato Base, pumpkin, bourbon, and molasses until mixture is smooth and uniform in color. Add the ginger, cinnamon, nutmeg, cloves and allspice and whisk until thoroughly incorporated. Place in a covered container and refrigerate until cold, 4 hours or overnight. Place the chopped maple cinnamon pecans or nut brittle in a covered container in the freezer. Chill a 2-quart metal bowl in the freezer.

Once the base has chilled, churn it in your home ice cream maker. When the gelato is done freezing scoop gelato into a cold bowl. Add the cold chopped pecans or nut brittle and caramel sauce and fold together so the pieces are evenly distributed. The caramel sauce will be a little difficult to pour out of the fridge but it should not be hot. Once combined cover the bowl and put in back into the freezer.

Yield: 50 oz. (about 3+ pints)

₰FRAGRANT SALTY NUTS₰

Paying homage to the timeless *Saturday Night Live* sketch, we've taken a cinnamon peanut base, thrown in a touch of salt, and folded in candied nuts. A perfect complement to the holiday favorite, "Schwetty Balls."

INGREDIENTS:

4 cups (32 oz. or 907g) Classic White Gelato Base, chilled

1 teaspoon (6g) sea salt

½ teaspoon (1⅔g) ground cinnamon

½ cup (4 oz. or 113g) peanut butter

⅛ cup (1 oz. or 28g) powdered sugar

½ cup (5 oz. or 142g) Maple Cinnamon Pecans or Nut Brittle

In a large bowl whisk together the Classic White Gelato Base, sea salt, cinnamon, peanut butter, and powdered sugar until mixture is smooth and uniform in color. Place in a covered container and refrigerate until cold, 4 hours or overnight. Chill a 2-quart metal bowl in the freezer. Place the maple nuts in a covered container in the freezer also

Once the base has chilled, churn it in your home ice cream maker. When the gelato is done freezing scoop gelato into the cold bowl. Add the cold maple pecans or nut brittle (chopped into ½-inch or 1-cm pieces) and fold together so the pieces are evenly distributed. Once combined put lid on stainless steel bowl and put in freezer.

Yield: 42 oz. (about 3 pints)

❧ GERMAN CHOCOLATE CAKE ❧

Chocolate coconut cake with pecans! Hansel and Gretel would not be able to refuse this gelato.

INGREDIENTS:

1 cup (8 oz. or 227g) Classic White Gelato Base, chilled

2 ¼ cups (18 oz. or 510g) Decadent Chocolate Gelato Base, chilled

1 can (15 oz. or 425g) Goya coconut cream

¼ cup (1½ oz. or 42g) cake flour

⅓ cup (2 oz. or 57g) powdered sugar

2 tablespoons (¼ oz. or 7g) pure vanilla extract

1 cup (2 oz. or 57g) toasted coconut flakes

¾ cup (3 oz. or 85g) chopped pecans

You may wish to toast the flour for several minutes to kill any potential bacteria. In a large bowl whisk together the Classic White Gelato Base, Decadent Chocolate Gelato Base, Goya coconut cream, cake flour, powdered sugar, and vanilla until mixture is smooth and uniform in color. Place in a covered container and refrigerate until cold, 4 hours or overnight. Chill a 2-quart metal bowl in the freezer. Place the coconut and pecans in a covered container in the freezer also.

Once the base has chilled, churn it in your home ice cream maker. When the gelato is done freezing scoop into the cold bowl. Add the cold maple pecans or nut brittle (chopped into ½-inch or 1-cm pieces) and fold together so the pieces are evenly distributed. Once combined put lid on stainless steel bowl and put in freezer.

Yield: 49 oz. (about 3+ pints)

{GROUND CHERRY}

Ground cherries are also known as Cape gooseberries or golden berries. You can now find them at supermarkets in-season and they grow in the wild in Maine. If you find them in the wild, they have a husk that must be removed like a tomatillo. They have a slightly firm texture and eat more like a soft orange with a thin, edible skin. They have a slight acidic flavor that is like pineapple or tart strawberry. Make this flavor and see if your family can guess what the secret ingredient is.

INGREDIENTS:

3 cups (24 oz. or 686g) Classic White Gelato Base, chilled

2 cups (12 oz. or 340g) ground cherries

⅓ cup (4 oz. or 120g) Sugar Syrup

1 tablespoon (½ oz. or 14g) lemon juice

½ teaspoon (¹/₇ oz. or 4.25g) sea salt

Place washed ground cherries, sugar syrup, and lemon juice in a blender and blend until smooth. In a large bowl whisk together the Classic White Gelato Base, ground cherries mixture, and sea salt until mixture is smooth and uniform in color. Place in a covered container and refrigerate until cold, 4 hours or overnight.

Once the base has chilled, churn it in your home ice cream maker.

Yield: 50 oz. (about 3 pints)

❧ SPECIAL HAZELNUT ☙

It didn't seem right to just call it "Hazelnut Gelato." After all, our hazelnuts come from the Piedmont region of Italy; thus, they're special. (You can use use hazelnuts from anywhere, and they'll still be just as special.) So I added the "Special" to point out our extra effort. I think the staff has grown weary of explaining it but it still sparks a daily conversation.

INGREDIENTS:

4 cups (32 oz. or 907g) Classic White Gelato Base, chilled

⅓ cup (3½ oz. or 99g) pure ground hazelnut butter

½ teaspoon (3g) sea salt

In a large bowl whisk together the Classic White Gelato Base, hazelnut butter and sea salt until mixture is smooth and uniform in color. Place in a covered container and refrigerate until cold, 4 hours or overnight.

Once the base has chilled, churn it in your home ice cream maker.

Yield: 35 oz. (about 2 pints)

❧ HAZELNUT DARK CHOCOLATE ☙

INGREDIENTS:

4 cups (32 oz. or 907g) Decadent Chocolate Gelato Base, chilled

⅓ cup (3 oz. or 85g) pure hazelnut butter

3 tablespoons (1 oz. or 28g) powdered sugar

In a large bowl whisk together the Decadent Chocolate Gelato Base, hazelnut butter, and powdered sugar until mixture is smooth and uniform in color. Place in a covered container and refrigerate until cold, 4 hours or overnight.

Once the base has chilled, churn it in your home ice cream maker.

Yield: 35 oz. (about 2 pints)

MYSTERY PINTS

A bedeviling question of any gelato shop is what to do with the leftovers? The gelato left in the pan at the end of the day is perfectly delicious, but we need the space for the next day. It was such a shame to throw it away, and the idea of giving it to employees to take home lasted a few weeks until everyone had all the gelato they ever needed (and growing waistlines).

Most shops will pack up the ends of pans into pints, label what's inside and try to sell them to customers, usually at some discount. We tried that, but couldn't sell them to save our lives. People would rather pay full price for a fresh pint than buy a day-old pint at half off. Plus, it created a lot of extra work; each pint had to be carefully labeled and we would end up with tons of shall-we-say "less in demand flavors" and sell through the "hot" flavors. Plus, people would expect us to keep flavors in stock at the discounted price. It was a real headache.

One night, I decided to combine a "hot" flavor with a "less hot" flavor in the same pint and call it a "mystery pint," with no label to indicate what was inside. I made them half price and waited to see what would happen. People were immediately intrigued and asked lots of questions: "So, really, what's inside?" I always claim to not remember.

Well, the idea was crazy enough that it worked and mystery pints flew off the shelves. We had to put a disclaimer on the pints and deal with a few issues. People are sad when we don't have enough odds and ends to make mystery pints. They have actually asked us to make mystery pints for them from the case! People also try to cheat by peeking under the lid!

The best mystery pint story is the couple who met at Gelato Fiasco and bonded over mystery pints and trying to guess what they were eating once they got home. We ended up catering their wedding and they gave mystery pints to all the guests as party favors.

A GELATO FIASCO ORIGINAL

MYSTERY PINT

Feeling lucky? At the end of each day, we make room for tomorrow's new flavors. Determined not to let good gelato and sorbetto go to waste, we pack otherwise perfectly delicious gelato into these pints. What's the catch? The contents of each pint are a MYSTERY...

$4.50

FINEST PRINT: WE DON'T RECALL WHAT'S INSIDE, SO FOLKS WITH ALLERGIES, EXTREME FLAVOR PREFERENCES, BAD LUCK, OR FINICKY TASTES SHOULDN'T TAKE CHANCES. NO RETURNS, TRADES, OR SWAPSIES.

⊰ HONEY GRAHAM ⊱

INGREDIENTS:

4 cups (32oz or 907g) Classic White Gelato Base,

1 teaspoon (2g) ground cinnamon

7 whole crackers, (4 oz. or 113g) graham crackers broken into ½-inch pieces

In a large bowl whisk together the Classic White Gelato Base, and vanilla until mixture is smooth and uniform in color. Place in a covered container and refrigerate until cold, 2 hours or overnight. Chill a 2-quart metal bowl in the freezer. Place the graham cracker pieces in a covered container in the freezer also.

Once the base has chilled, churn it in your home ice cream maker. When the gelato is done freezing scoop gelato into the cold bowl. Add the cold graham cracker pieces and fold together so the pieces are evenly distributed. Once combined put lid on stainless steel bowl and put in freezer.

Yield: 36 oz. (about 2+ pints)

• •

⊰ KEY LIME PIE ⊱

INGREDIENTS:

4 cups (32 oz. or 907g) Classic White Gelato Base, chilled

¼ cup (4 oz. or 113g) lime juice; key lime is best, if available

¼ cup (1 oz. or 28g) powdered sugar

½ cup (1 oz. or 28g) skim milk powder

2 teaspoons (10g) pure vanilla extract

7 whole crackers, (4 oz. or 113g) graham crackers broken into ½-inch/1cm pieces

⅓ cup (2 oz. or 57g) Sugar Syrup

In a large bowl whisk together the Classic White Gelato Base, key lime juice, powdered sugar, skim milk powder and vanilla until mixture is smooth and uniform in color. Place in a covered container and refrigerate until cold, 4 hours or overnight. Pour the graham cracker pieces into a zip top plastic bag. Drizzle them with sugar syrup. Seal the bag and shake to coat all of the graham cracker pieces with syrup. Open a corner of the bag and compress it to remove excess air. Flatten the bag and place it along with a 2-quart metal bowl in the freezer.

Once the base has chilled, churn it in your home ice cream maker. When the gelato is done churning, scoop it into the cold bowl. Add the cold syrup coated graham cracker pieces and fold together so the pieces are evenly distributed. Once combined cover the stainless steel bowl and return it to the freezer.

Yield: 44 oz. (about 3 pints)

⁅ LAVENDER HONEY ⁆

Jeni's Spendid Ice Cream's book on making ice cream at home was a revelation (and an inspiration as we set out to write a cookbook about gelato at home). She perfectly captured the ice cream and gelato maker's approach in viewing ingredients in terms of their components and using science to build flavor and texture by recombining each component carefully and thoughtfully. Jeni is brilliant at delivering flavor and a favorite trick of her's is using essential oils—and not just the essential oil of the flavor you'd expect. In this case it's not only the lavender, but also the sweet orange essential oil. The orange note heightens the flavors and really pulls it all together in this recipe.

INGREDIENTS:

4 cups (32 oz. or 907g) Classic White Gelato Base, chilled

2 drops lavender essential oil

1 drop sweet orange essential oil

¼ cup (3 oz. or 85g plus extra for drizzling on top later) honey; choose a bold, dark variety like Tupelo if you can. The honey flavor will be subtle but needs to stand up to the other flavors.

In a large bowl whisk together the Classic White Gelato Base and honey until mixture is smooth and uniform in color. Place in a covered container and refrigerate until cold, 4 hours or overnight.

Once the base has chilled, churn it in your home ice cream maker. As the gelato begins to form but before it gets too hard, drop the essential oils into the mixture.

Best eaten immediately with a little drizzle of extra honey.

Yield: 32 oz. (about 2 pints)

LEMON BUTTERMILK SHORTBREAD

INGREDIENTS:

- 3 cups (24 oz. or 680g) Classic White Gelato Base, chilled
- 1 cup (8 oz. or 227g) real buttermilk (we like to use Kate's of Maine)
- Zest of 2 lemons
- 2 tablespoons (28g) pure vanilla extract
- ¼ cup (2 oz. or 57g) plain unsweetened Greek yogurt
- ¼ cup (2 oz. or 57g) lemon juice—approximately the juice of two lemons
- ½ cup (1 oz. or 28g) skim milk powder
- ½ cup (1 oz. or 28g) powdered sugar
- ½ cup (4 oz. or 113g) shortbread broken into dime sized pieces
- ⅓ cup (2 oz. or 57g) Sugar Syrup

In a large bowl whisk together the buttermilk, lemon zest, vanilla, yogurt, lemon juice, skim milk powder, and powdered sugar until mixture is smooth and uniform in color. Whisk in the Classic White Gelato base. Place in a covered container and refrigerate until cold, 4 hours or overnight. Pour the shortbread pieces into a zip top plastic bag. Drizzle them with the sugar syrup. Seal the bag and shake gently to coat all of the cookie pieces with syrup. Open a corner of the bag and compress it to remove excess air. Flatten the bag and place it along with a 2-quart metal bowl in the freezer.

Once the base has chilled, churn it in your home ice cream maker. When the gelato is finished churning, scoop it into the cold bowl and fold in the pieces of sugar syrup coated shortbread. Cover and return it to the freezer.

Yield: 42 oz. (about 3 pints)

❧ MADAGASCAR VANILLA BEAN ☙

Vanilla may seem plain, but it has always been something we have chosen to focus on. If you are going to master gelato, you have to start by mastering the basics. Throughout our years in the industry, we have seen the price of vanilla fluctuate — most recently due to a series of tornadoes in Madagascar. Even so, we have never let our standards slip. Artificial vanilla is just gross. We will always invest in the real deal.

INGREDIENTS:

4 cups (32 oz. or 907g) Rich Yellow Gelato Base

1 Madagascar vanilla bean

1 tablespoon (14g) pure vanilla extract

Prepare the vanilla bean by slicing it in half lengthwise. Laying it flat on a cutting board, scrape the tiny seeds out with a paring knife and place them in a small dish. Stir in two tablespoons (14g) of gelato base until the vanilla bean seeds are evenly distributed. Reserve the vanilla bean pod for another recipe.

In a large bowl whisk together the Rich Yellow Gelato Base, vanilla bean seed mixture and vanilla extract until mixture is smooth and uniform in color. Place in a covered container and refrigerate until cold, 4 hours or overnight.

Once the base has chilled, churn it in your home ice cream maker.

Yield: 32 oz. (about 2 pints)

MAGIC BAR

Just like the bar cookies from your favorite church supper cookbook. All the chewy gooey flavors rolled up into one delicious gelato.

INGREDIENTS:

3½ cups (28 oz. or 794g) Classic White or Rich Yellow Gelato Base, chilled

¼ cup (4 oz. or 113g) sweetened condensed milk

¼ cup (4 oz. or 113g) Goya coconut cream

½ cup (4 oz. or 113g) skim milk

1 tablespoon (14g) pure vanilla extract

1 teaspoon (6g) sea salt

6 whole crackers, (3 oz. or 85g) graham crackers broken into ½-inch pieces

½ cup (3 oz .or 85g) chocolate chunks

½ cup (3 oz. or 85g) chopped pecans

In a large bowl whisk together the Classic White Gelato Base, sweetened condensed milk, coconut cream, skim milk, vanilla, and sea salt until mixture is smooth and uniform in color. Place in a covered container and refrigerate until cold, 4 hours or overnight. Pour the graham cracker pieces, chocolate chunks and chopped pecans into a zip top plastic bag. Open a corner of the bag and compress it to remove excess air. Flatten the bag, seal it and place it along with a 2-quart metal bowl in the freezer.

Once the base has chilled, churn it in your home ice cream maker. When the gelato is finished churning, scoop it into the cold bowl and fold in the pieces of graham crackers, chocolate chunks and chopped pecans until they are evenly distributed. Cover and return it to the freezer.

Yield: 49 oz. (about 3+ pints)

⟨ MAPLE SAP TAP ⟩

Buckets are saddled against maple trees across Maine every March, collecting precious sap to be boiled into syrup. Maple Sap Tap Gelato is a special sugarhouse delight made with rich Maine maple syrup and our house-made maple walnut toffee.

INGREDIENTS:

4 cups (32 oz. or 907g) Classic White Gelato Base, chilled

$^1\!/_6$ cup (2 oz. or 57g) pure Maine maple syrup

2 tablespoons (½ oz. or 14g) molasses

½ cup (5 oz. or 142g) Maple Cinnamon Pecans or Nut Brittle

In a large bowl whisk together the Classic White Gelato Base, maple syrup, and molasses until mixture is smooth and uniform in color. Place in a covered container and refrigerate until cold, 4 hours or overnight. Pour the pecans into a zip top plastic bag. Seal and place it along with a 2-quart metal bowl in the freezer.

Once the base has chilled, churn it in your home ice cream maker. When the gelato is finished churning, scoop it into the cold bowl and fold in the cold maple cinnamon pecans. Cover and return it to the freezer.

Yield: 39 oz. (about 2+ pints)

SAFE, INCLUSIVE PLACES

Our stores are inclusive and vibrant spots for people to share desserts and coffee. We're proud that our stores are comfortable, happy gathering places.

❦MASCARPONE FIG❧

The marriage of figs in all their forms and mascarpone make this sweet, multifaceted, delectable gelato sing like a resonant tenor at the opera: *Fig-aro! Fiiiig-aro!*

INGREDIENTS:

3½ cups (28 oz. or 794g) Classic White Gelato Base

8 oz. tub (227g) mascarpone cheese

¼ cup (2 oz. or 57g) brown sugar

Seeds from one vanilla bean

¼ cup (2 oz. or 57g) Fig Fig Fig Variegate

In a large bowl whisk together the warm Classic White Gelato Base, mascarpone cheese, brown sugar, and vanilla bean seeds until mixture is smooth and uniform in color. Place in a covered container and refrigerate until cold, 4 hours or overnight. Chill the fig variegate. Place a 2-quart metal bowl in the freezer.

Once the base has chilled, churn it in your home ice cream maker. When the gelato is finished churning, scoop it into the cold bowl and fold in the fig variegate until it is swirled throughout. Cover and return it to the freezer.

Yield: 39 oz. (about 3 pints)

MASCARPONE PISTACHIO CARAMEL

This is probably our most popular pint flavor and it was based on a customer suggestion at the Brunswick shop. It reminds us of the filling of a Sicilian cannoli. It's got the right amount of pistachio pieces and globs of salty caramel sauce juxtaposed against the creamy mascarpone cheese background.

INGREDIENTS:

3½ cups (28 oz. or 794g) Classic White Gelato Base

8-oz. tub (227g) mascarpone cheese

¼ cup (2 oz. or 57g) brown sugar

Seeds from one vanilla bean

¼ cup (3 oz. or 85g) Smooth Caramel Sauce

¼ cup (1½ oz. or 42g) chopped pistachios

In a large bowl whisk together the warm Classic White Gelato Base, mascarpone cheese, brown sugar, and vanilla bean seeds until mixture is smooth and uniform in color. Place in a covered container and refrigerate until cold, 4 hours or overnight. Pour the chopped pistachios into a zip top plastic bag and place it along with a 2-quart metal bowl in the freezer.

Once the base has chilled, churn it in your home ice cream maker. When the gelato is finished churning, scoop it into the cold bowl and fold in the smooth caramel and chopped pistachios until they are thoroughly incorporated. Cover and return it to the freezer.

Yield: 44 oz. (about 3 pints)

⊰MILK CHOCOLATE PRETZEL⊱

INGREDIENTS:

4 cups (32 oz. or 907g) Decadent Chocolate Gelato Base, chilled

1 teaspoon (6g) sea salt

1 cup (5 oz. or 142g) chopped chocolate covered pretzels

In a large bowl whisk together the warm Decadent Chocolate Gelato Base and sea salt until mixture is smooth and uniform in color. Place in a covered container and refrigerate until cold, 4 hours or overnight. Chill the chopped chocolate covered pretzels in a zip top plastic bag. Place a 2-quart metal bowl in the freezer.

Once the base has chilled, churn it in your home ice cream maker. When the gelato is finished churning, scoop it into the cold bowl and fold in the cold chopped chocolate covered pretzels until it is swirled throughout. Cover and return it to the freezer.

Yield: 37 oz. (about 2 pints)

❧ MINT CHOCOLATE CHUNK ❧

INGREDIENTS:

4 cups (32 oz. or 907g) Classic White Gelato Base, chilled

2 teaspoons (10g) pure peppermint extract

½ cup (4 oz. or 113g) chocolate chunks

In a large bowl whisk together the Classic White Gelato Base, and peppermint extract. Pour into a covered container and refrigerate until cold, 4 hours or overnight. Place the chocolate chunks in a zip top plastic bag. Chill the chocolate chunks and a 2-quart metal bowl in the freezer.

Once the base has chilled, churn it in your home ice cream maker. When the gelato is finished churning, scoop it into the cold bowl and fold in the cold chocolate chunks until it is swirled throughout. Cover and return it to the freezer.

Yield: 36 oz. (about 2 pints)

⧼ MINT COOKIES AND CREAM ⧽

INGREDIENTS:

4 cups (32 oz. or 907g) Classic White Gelato Base, chilled

2 teaspoons (10g) peppermint extract

1 cup (5 oz. or 142g) cream-filled chocolate cookie sandwiches, coarsely chopped

In a large bowl whisk together the Classic White Gelato Base and vanilla until mixture is smooth and uniform in color. Place in a covered container and refrigerate until cold, 4 hours or overnight. Place the chocolate cookie sandwich pieces in a plastic zip top bag or airtight container in the freezer. Close the zip top bag, pressing out as much air as you can. Place it and a 2-quart metal bowl in the freezer to chill.

Once the base has chilled, churn it in your home ice cream maker. When the gelato is done freezing scoop it into the cold bowl. Fold the cold chocolate cookie pieces into the frozen gelato until evenly distributed.

Yield: 37 oz. (about 2 pints)

❧ MOLASSES PEPPERMINT ❧

Josh's childhood flavor fantasy finally came true. And guess what? Grown-ups love this unexpected juxtaposition of flavors!

INGREDIENTS:

4 cups (32 oz. or 907g) Classic White Gelato Base, chilled

1 teaspoons (5g) peppermint extract

¼ cup (3 oz. or 85g) molasses

Optional: 2 medium (3 oz. or 142g) candy canes, finely chopped

In a large bowl whisk together the Classic White Gelato Base, peppermint extract, and molasses until mixture is smooth and uniform in color. Place in a covered container and refrigerate until cold, 4 hours or overnight. If you're adding candy canes, place them in a zip-top plastic bag and place with a 2-quart metal bowl in the freezer to chill.

Once the base has chilled, churn it in your home ice cream maker. At this point the gelato is perfectly complete. If you'd like to add the candy cane pieces here, feel free to! They do add to the beauty. Just be sure to chop them finely or run them through your food processor and remove any belligerent chunks that don't want to cooperate. Fold the optional candy cane pieces into the frozen gelato until evenly distributed. Once combined cover the bowl and return it to the freezer.

Yield: 38 oz. (about 2 pints)

❧NEEDHAM❧

Needhams are a Maine potato-coconut candy dipped in chocolate. The potatoes act as the binder that holds the coconut together. Wilbur's Chocolates, just down the street from our flagship store, creates a homemade, traditional Needham from a recipe handed down through the generations. They make them from Maine potatoes and locally infused vanilla. The best of the best rolled into one gelato!

INGREDIENTS:

3 cups (24 oz. or 680g) Classic White Gelato Base, chilled

1 can (15 oz. or 425g) Goya coconut cream

¼ cup (1 oz. or 28g) toasted coconut flakes

⅓ cup (4 oz. or 113g) coarsely chopped Needhams candies

In a large bowl whisk together the Classic White Gelato Base, coconut cream, and vanilla until mixture is smooth and uniform in color. Place in a covered container and refrigerate until cold, 4 hours or overnight. Place the toasted coconut and Needhams candy pieces together in a plastic zip top bag or airtight container. Close the zip top bag, pressing out as much air as you can. Place it and a 2-quart metal bowl in the freezer to chill.

Once the base has chilled, churn it in your home ice cream maker. When the gelato is done freezing, scoop it into the cold bowl. Fold the cold toasted coconut and Needhams candy pieces into the frozen gelato until evenly distributed. Once combined, cover the bowl and return it to the freezer.

Yield: 44 oz. (about 2 pints)

ᓫNUTTY BAILEY'Sᕽ

INGREDIENTS:

4 cups (32 oz. or 907g) Classic White Gelato Base, chilled

¼ cup (2 oz. or 57g) Bailey's Irish Cream liqueur

2 tablespoons (1½ oz. or 42g) Frangelico liqueur

In a large bowl whisk together the Classic White Gelato Base, Bailey's, and Frangelico until mixture is smooth and uniform in color. Place in a covered container and refrigerate until cold, 4 hours or overnight.

Once the base has chilled, churn it in your home ice cream maker.

Yield: 35 oz. (about 2 pints)

No Limits

When building out our stores and customer service experience, we've always tried to say "yes" more often than "no!" A couple of interesting anecdotes illustrate this point. When one of our first customers asked us how many

flavors they could sample, we hadn't thought about that question, so we just said "as many as you want!"

Likewise, another customer in that first week wanted to put several flavors in a dish, and asked what the limit was for the smallest size. We hadn't thought about that question either, so we just again said "as many as you want!"

That just became the custom. The tradition really became a bedrock of our hospitality and word spread about how fun a visit to Gelato Fiasco could be. We often overhear longtime customers telling new customers with great delight, "you can try as many as you want before you decide!" Folks are often amazed that staff will squeeze five, six, or seven flavors into a treat dish. It's often the simplest things that make such a big difference.

❧ OLIVE OIL ❧

INGREDIENTS:

2 cups (16 oz. or 454g) Classic White Gelato Base, chilled

2 cups (16 oz. or 454g) skim milk

2 tablespoons (2½ oz. or 71g) olive oil

1 cup (2 oz. or 57g) skim milk powder

¾ cup (4 oz. or 113g) powdered sugar

In a large bowl whisk together the Classic White Gelato Base, skim milk, olive oil, skim milk powder and powdered sugar until mixture is smooth and uniform in color. Place in a covered container and refrigerate until cold, 4 hours or overnight.

Once the base has chilled, churn it in your home ice cream maker.

Yield: 44 oz. (about 2 pints)

• •

❧ PANNA COTTA ❧

Panna cotta means "cooked cream" in Italian, and the Italian panna cotta dessert is basically gelatin flavored with milk. It has a silky, dense texture and a sweet milk flavor. You'll find a panna cotta gelato flavor in most any gelato shop in Italy; our version is a take on the classic, but we use two types of caramel to replicate the subtle dairy and caramelized sugar aspects of the dessert.

INGREDIENTS:

4 cups (32 oz. or 907g) Classic White Gelato Base, chilled

2 tablespoons (1 oz. or 28g) Caramel Sea Salt Caramel

2 tablespoons (1 oz. or 28g) Dark Chocolate Caramel Sea Salt Caramel

2 teaspoons (10g) pure vanilla extract

½ teaspoon (2g) sea salt

In a large bowl whisk together the Classic White Gelato Base, caramel sea salt caramel, dark chocolate caramel sea salt caramel, salt, and vanilla until mixture is smooth and uniform in color. Place in a covered container and refrigerate until cold, 4 hours or overnight.

Once the base has chilled, churn it in your home ice cream maker.

Yield: 34 oz. (about 2 pints)

❧ PUMPKIN PIE ❧

The spices in this gelato were inspired by Josh's grandmother's pumpkin pie recipe. Customers in our shops have debated over the past ten years whether it's best made with or without crust pieces. To put it to the test, simply crush and twist in some gingersnap cookies at the end.

INGREDIENTS:

3 cups (24 oz. or 680g) Classic White Gelato Base

1 cup (8 oz. or 227g) pureed pumpkin (we like One Pie brand because it's from Maine and it's what Josh's grandma used)

⅓ cup (4 oz. or 113g) molasses

1 teaspoon (2g) ground ginger

1½ teaspoons (3g) cinnamon

1 teaspoon (2g) nutmeg

¼ teaspoon (½g) ground cloves

¼ teaspoon (½g) ground allspice

In a large bowl whisk together the Classic White Gelato Base, pumpkin, and molasses until mixture is smooth and uniform in color. Add the ginger, cinnamon, nutmeg, cloves and allspice and whisk until thoroughly incorporated. Place in a covered container and refrigerate until cold, 4 hours or overnight.

Once the base has chilled, churn it in your home ice cream maker according to the manufacturer's instructions.

Yield: 36 oz. (about 3+ pints)

PEANUT BUTTER DREAM

Bruno has always had a flair for the dramatic when it comes to names. Well, that's not actually true at all—he normally just names every ingredient in a given flavor. Creativity aside, in this case, it was just too good to name it anything else.

INGREDIENTS:

- 4 cups (32 oz. or 907g) Classic White Gelato Base, chilled
- ½ cup (4 oz. or 113g) pure smooth peanut butter
- ½ teaspoon (3g) sea salt

In a large bowl whisk together the Classic White Gelato Base, peanut butter, and sea salt until mixture is smooth and uniform in color. Place in a covered container and refrigerate until cold, 4 hours or overnight.

Once the base has chilled, churn it in your home ice cream maker.

Yield: 38 oz. (about 2 pints)

• •

PEANUT BUTTER SRIRACHA

Is it nutty, salty, or spicy? Smooth or crunchy? This captivating combination of peanut butter, sriracha, and salted peanuts will leave your taste buds crazy in love.

INGREDIENTS:

- 4 cups (32 oz. or 907g) Classic White Gelato Base, chilled
- 2 tablespoons (1½ oz. or 42g) sriracha
- ½ cup (4 oz. or 113g) pure smooth peanut butter
- ½ teaspoon (3g) sea salt
- ⅓ cup (2 oz. or 56g) salted peanuts, coursely chopped and chilled

In a large bowl whisk together the Classic White Gelato Base, sriracha, smooth peanut butter, and sea salt until mixture is smooth and uniform in color. Place in a covered container and refrigerate until cold, 4 hours or overnight.

Place the peanuts in a plastic zip top bag or airtight container, sealing out as much air as you can. Place it and a 2-quart metal bowl in the freezer to chill.

Once the gelato has chilled, churn it in your home ice cream maker. When the gelato is done freezing, scoop it into the cold bowl. Fold the peanuts into the frozen gelato until evenly distributed. Once combined, cover the bowl and return it to the freezer.

Once the base has chilled, churn it in your home ice cream maker.

Yield: 35 oz. (about 2+ pints)

₰PEANUT BUTTER STRACCIATELLA₰

This gelato takes creamy peanut butter to new heights with abundant chocolate slivers and a pinch of sea salt. If you prefer using only semi-sweet or bittersweet chocolate, feel free to use 4 oz. of either one.

INGREDIENTS:

4 cups (32 oz. or 907g) Classic White Gelato Base

½ cup (4 oz. or 113g) pure smooth peanut butter

½ teaspoon (3g) sea salt

½ cup (3 oz. or 85g) semi-sweet chocolate chips

2 tablespoons (1 oz. or 28g) bittersweet chocolate chips

In a large bowl whisk together the Classic White Gelato Base, peanut butter and sea salt until mixture is smooth and uniform in color. Place in a covered container and refrigerate until cold, 4 hours or overnight. Place a medium sized stainless steel bowl in the freezer to chill.

Once the base has chilled, churn it in your home ice cream maker.

While the gelato is churning, in a double boiler set over simmering water, melt the semi-sweet and bittersweet chocolate bits together. Allow chocolate to cool to room temperature, while it still remains fluid.

When the gelato is has finished churning, scoop it into the cold bowl. Cover the bowl and place it back in the freezer for 30 minutes to give the gelato time to freeze. Drizzle the melted chocolate over the frozen gelato and as it cools and firms, using two spoons, break the pieces of chocolate up into small chunks. Stir the chocolate chunks into the finished gelato.

Yield: 38 oz. (about 3 pints)

⊰ SICILIAN PISTACHIO ⊱

We have always incorporated gorgeous imported pistachios from Sicily in this recipe. See the resource section for more information.

INGREDIENTS:

4 cups (32 oz. or 907g) Classic White Gelato Base, chilled

⅓ cup (3½ oz. or 99g) pure ground pistachio butter

½ teaspoon (3g) sea salt

In a large bowl whisk together the Classic White Gelato Base, pistachio butter, and sea salt until mixture is smooth and uniform in color. Place in a covered container and refrigerate until cold, 4 hours or overnight.

Once the base has chilled, churn it in your home ice cream maker.

Yield: 35 oz. (about 2+ pints)

• •

⊰ SINGLE MALT SCOTCH ⊱

INGREDIENTS:

4 cups (32 oz. or 907g) Classic White Gelato Base, chilled

1½ tablespoons (¾ oz. or 21g) pure vanilla extract

½ cup (4 oz. or 113g) single malt scotch

In a large bowl whisk together the Classic White Gelato Base, vanilla, and scotch until mixture is smooth and uniform in color. Place in a covered container and refrigerate until cold, 4 hours or overnight.

Once the base has chilled, churn it in your home ice cream maker.

Yield: 36 oz. (about 2 pints)

❧ SPIKED EGGNOG ❧

This eggnog gelato is a throwback to merry days of old. It's laced with just a splash of marsala and bourbon to keep it real. Enjoy!

INGREDIENTS:

4 cups (32 oz. or 907g) Rich Yellow Gelato Base

1 whole nutmeg seed, ground fine in a small electric grinder or by hand

1 tablespoon (½ oz. or 14g) bourbon

2 tablespoons (1 oz. or 28g) marsala wine

In a large bowl whisk together the Rich Yellow Gelato Base, fresh ground nutmeg, bourbon, and marsala until mixture is smooth and uniform in color. Place in a covered container and refrigerate until cold, 4 hours or overnight.

Once the base has chilled, churn it in your home ice cream maker.

Yield: 40 oz. (about 2.5 pints)

⊰ STRACCIATELLA ⊱

We make Straciatella gelato almost every day at our shops. The name means "shredded" in Italian; we literally use gelato spades to shred molten chocolate that starts to reharden into little flecks of chocolate. If you prefer using only semi-sweet or bittersweet chocolate, feel free to use four ounces of either.

INGREDIENTS:

4 cups (32 oz. or 907g) Classic White Gelato Base

2 teaspoons (10g) pure vanilla extract

½ cup (3 oz. or 85g) semi sweet chocolate chips

3 tablespoons (1 oz. or 28g) bittersweet chocolate chips

In a large bowl whisk together the Classic White Gelato Base, and vanilla until mixture is smooth and uniform in color. Place in a covered container and refrigerate until cold, 2 hours or overnight. Place a 2-quart stainless steel bowl in the freezer to chill.

Once the base has chilled, churn it in your home ice cream maker. While the gelato is churning, in a double boiler set over simmering water, melt the semi-sweet and bitter-sweet chocolate bits together. Allow chocolate to cool to room temperature, while it still remains fluid.

When the gelato has finished churning, scoop it into the cold bowl. Cover the bowl and place it back in the freezer for 30 minutes to give the gelato time to freeze. After 30 minutes remove the bowl from the freezer and drizzle the slightly cooled, melted chocolate over the frozen gelato. As it cools and firms, using two spoons, break the pieces of chocolate up into small chunks. Stir the chocolate chunks into the finished gelato. Once combined cover the stainless steel bowl and return it to the freezer.

Yield: 36 oz. (about 3 pints)

꧁ SWEET RESURGAM ꧂

Named for Portland's motto, which means, "I shall rise again," this is a burnt sugar almond gelato with swirls of salted caramel and chocolate chips. First created to celebrate the opening of our Old Port store, this flavor was so beloved by customers that we had to keep it around.

INGREDIENTS:

4 cups (32 oz. or 907g) Classic White Gelato Base

2 tablespoons (1 oz. or 28g) Dark Chocolate Caramel Sea Salt Caramel

2 tablespoons (1 oz. or 28g) almond butter

⅛ cup (1 oz. or 28g) powdered sugar

1 teaspoon (6g) sea salt

¾ cup (4 oz. or 113g) chocolate chunks

¼ cup (3 oz. or 85g) Smooth Caramel

In a large bowl combine the Classic White Gelato Base, Dark Chocolate Sea Salt Caramel, almond butter, powdered sugar, and sea salt. Stir until smooth, then return it to the refrigerator. Continue to chill until cold, another 2 hours or overnight. Place the chocolate chunks in a covered container in the freezer. Chill a 2-quart metal bowl in the freezer.

Once the base has chilled, churn it in your home ice cream maker. When the gelato is done freezing scoop it into the cold bowl. Add the cold chocolate chunks, and smooth caramel. Fold together so the chocolate chunks and caramel are evenly distributed. Once combined put a lid on the stainless steel bowl and return it to the freezer.

Yield: 45 oz. (about 3 pints)

❧ TOASTED COCONUT ❧

Our smooth and creamy coconut gelato is layered with gently toasted coconut flakes. We are unabashedly nuts about it.

INGREDIENTS:

3 cups (24 oz. or 680g) Classic White Gelato Base, chilled

1 can (15 oz. or 425g) Goya coconut cream

¾ cup (2 oz. or 57g) toasted coconut flakes

In a large bowl whisk together the Classic White Gelato Base, and Goya coconut cream until mixture is smooth and uniform in color. Place in a covered container and refrigerate until cold, 4 hours or overnight. Place the toasted coconut flakes in a zip top plastic bag and put it and a 2-quart metal bowl in the freezer to chill.

Once the base has chilled, churn it in your home ice cream maker. When the gelato has finished churning, fold in the toasted coconut flakes. Once combined put a lid on the stainless steel bowl and return it to the freezer.

Yield: 41 oz. (about 3+ pints)

⋵ TIRAMISU ⋺

Layers of espresso-soaked ladyfingers in a rich custard gelato.

INGREDIENTS:

4 cups (32 oz. or 907g) Rich Yellow Gelato Base

¼ cup (2 oz. or 57g) marsala wine

1 dozen (3 oz. or 85g) broken up ladyfingers

3 tablespoons (2 oz. or 57g) Sugar Syrup

2 tablespoons (¼ oz. or 7g) of cocoa powder

Stir the marsala into the warm gelato base. Place in a covered container and refrigerate 4 hours or overnight. Put the chopped ladyfingers into a zip top plastic bag. Pour in the 2 oz. sugar syrup and shake the bag until the pieces of ladyfingers are coated. Sprinkle the cocoa powder over the sugar syrup coated ladyfingers and shake gently again to coat. Close the zip top bag, pressing out as much air as you can. Place it and a 2-quart metal bowl in the freezer to chill.

Once the base has chilled, churn it in your home ice cream maker. When the gelato is done freezing scoop it into the cold bowl. Add the sugar syrup and cocoa coated ladyfinger pieces and fold together. Once combined put a lid on the stainless steel bowl and return it to the freezer.

Yield: 39 oz (about 3 pints)

❧TORCHED MARSHMALLOW S'MORE❧

An Acadia campfire classic: Graham crackers accented by pieces of Hershey's chocolate bars and gently toasted marshmallows.

INGREDIENTS:

4 cups (32 oz. or 907g) Classic White Gelato Base

1 teaspoon (2g) ground cinnamon

⅔ cup (4 oz. or 113g) semi-sweet chocolate chunks

~6½ (3½ oz. or 99g) whole graham crackers

1½ cups (2 oz. or 57g) torched mini marshmallows

Whisk the cinnamon into the classic white gelato base. Place in a covered container and chill 2 hours or overnight. Pulse the graham crackers in a food processor until finely ground. You can place the crackers in a zip top bag, pressing all the air out, sealing the bag and crush with a rolling pin until you've got a finely ground crumb. Place the chocolate chunks, graham cracker crumbs, and torched marshmallows together in a zip top bag. Place them and a 2-quart metal bowl in the freezer.

Once the base has chilled, churn it in your home ice cream maker. When the gelato is done freezing scoop it into the cold bowl. Add the cold chocolate chunks, graham cracker crumbs, and torched marshmallows. Fold together so all of the chunks are evenly distributed. Once combined put lid on stainless steel bowl and put in freezer.

Yield: 41 oz. (about 3 pints)

ꗈ TURKISH COFFEE ꗈ

INGREDIENTS:

5 cups (40 oz. or 1134g) Classic White Gelato Base

1¼ cups (4 oz. or 113g) ground coffee

2 teaspoons (10g) pure vanilla extract

½ teaspoon (1g) ground black pepper

2 teaspoons (4g) ground cardamom

In a large bowl whisk together the Classic White Gelato Base, and ground coffee. Place the mixture in the refrigerator to steep for 2 hours. Strain the mixture and discard solids. Add vanilla, black pepper and cardamom, stirring until mixture is smooth and uniform in color. Place in a covered container and refrigerate until cold, 2 more hours or overnight.

Once the base has chilled, churn it in your home ice cream maker.

Yield: 44 oz. (about 3 pints)

ꗈ VANILLA BEAN CRANBERRY ꗈ TRUFFLE

INGREDIENTS:

4 cups (32 oz. or 907g) Classic White Gelato Base

1½ tablespoons (¾ oz. or 21g) pure vanilla extract

½ cup (3 oz. or 113g) Homemade Chocolate Truffle pieces or chocolate chips

⅓ cup (4 oz. or 113g) cold cranberry jam

In a large bowl whisk together the Classic White Gelato Base and vanilla until mixture is smooth and uniform in color. Place in a covered container and refrigerate until cold, 2 hours or overnight. Place the chocolate chunks in a covered container along with a 2-quart metal bowl in the freezer.

Once the base has chilled, churn it in your home ice cream maker. When the gelato is done churning scoop it into the cold bowl. Add the cold chocolate truffle pieces, and cranberry jam. Fold together so the truffle pieces and jam are evenly distributed. Once combined put lid on stainless steel bowl and put in freezer.

Yield: 39 oz. (about 3 pints)

VANILLA MALT

This one just might unravel the very fabric of the space-time continuum. Malt powder turns rich and creamy vanilla gelato into a classic throwback dessert best consumed with your sweetie by your side, two spoons, and something special on the jukebox.

INGREDIENTS:

4 cups (32 oz. and 907g) Classic White Gelato Base

2 teaspoons (10g) pure vanilla extract

1 cup (5 oz. or 142g) Carnation malted milk powder

In a large bowl whisk together the Classic White Gelato Base, vanilla, and Carnation malted milk powder until mixture is smooth and uniform in color. Place in a covered container and refrigerate until cold, 4 hours or overnight.

Once the base has chilled, churn it in your home ice cream maker.

Yield: 37 oz. (about 3 pints)

WAFFLE CONE

INGREDIENTS:

4 cups (32 oz. or 907g) Classic White Gelato Base

2 teaspoons (10g) pure vanilla extract

½ teaspoon (1g) ground cinnamon

1 cup (5 oz. or 142g) waffle cones broken into ½-inch/1-cm pieces

3 tablespoons (2 oz. or 57g) sugar syrup

In a large bowl whisk together the Classic White Gelato Base, vanilla and cinnamon. Place in a covered container and refrigerate until cold, 2 hours or overnight. Put the waffle cone pieces into a zip top plastic bag. Pour in the sugar syrup and shake the bag until the pieces of cone are coated. Close the zip top bag, pressing out as much air as you can. Place it and a 2-quart metal bowl in the freezer to chill.

Once the base has chilled, churn it in your home ice cream maker. When the gelato is done churning scoop it into the cold bowl. Add the sugar syrup coated waffle cone pieces and fold together. Once combined put a lid on the stainless steel bowl and return it to the freezer.

Yield: 39 oz. (about 3 pints)

⟨WAKE N' BACON⟩

Good morning, Sunshine! You'll be ready to rise and shine with this: pancakes and bacon topped with pure Maine maple syrup. Delicious any time of day.

INGREDIENTS:

4 cups (32 oz. or 907g) Classic White Gelato Base

½ cup (2 oz. or 60g) cake flour

½ cup (3 oz. 85g) pure Maine maple syrup

½ cup (2 oz. 57g) molasses

1 tablespoon (14g) pure vanilla extract

1 cup (4 oz. or 113g) Roasted Candied Maple Bacon chopped into ½-inch pieces

You may wish toast the flour for several minutes to kill any potential bacteria. In a large bowl whisk together the Classic White Gelato Base, cake flour, maple syrup, molasses, and vanilla until mixture is smooth and uniform in color. Place in a covered container and refrigerate until cold, 4 hours or overnight. Place the chopped up candied bacon in a zip top plastic bag. Put it and a 2-quart metal bowl in the freezer to chill.

Once the base has chilled, churn it in your home ice cream maker. When the gelato is done churning, scoop it into the cold bowl. Add the cold chopped up candied bacon and fold together. Do not over mix. Cover and quickly return bowl to the freezer.

Yield: 43 oz. (about 3 pints)

❧ WHOOPIE PIE ❧

Whoopie pies are traditionally two soft, chocolate, cake-y cookies sandwiched around a light fluffy vanilla filling. Here's our take.

INGREDIENTS:

4 cups (32 oz. or 907g) Classic White Gelato Base

2 teaspoons (10g) pure vanilla extract

1 (6 oz. or 170g) chopped up whoopie pie—about one medium (4-inch) pie

In a large bowl whisk together the Classic White Gelato Base, and vanilla until mixture is smooth and uniform in color. Place in a covered container and refrigerate until cold, 2 hours or overnight. Chop up the whoopie pie into ½-inch pieces. Keep in mind that the softer the whoopie pie, the more likely it is going to turn into cake crumbs—not a bad thing—the bigger the pieces, the more likely there will be chunks of whoopie pie in your gelato. Place the chopped up whoopie pie in a zip top plastic bag. Put it and a 2-quart metal bowl in the freezer to chill.

Once the base has chilled, churn it in your home ice cream maker. When the gelato is done freezing, scoop it into the cold bowl. Add the cold chopped up whoopie pie and fold together. Do not over mix. Cover and return bowl to the freeze

Yield: 38 oz. (about 3 pints)

THE FROZEN CODE

Sometime in our first winter business became very, very slow. So we had a meeting with the whole team about what we might do and came up with the idea for some sort of promotion so that when it was below a certain temperature customers got a discount. Bruno suggested, "What if we just make it 1% off for every degree under 32," so, if the temperature is 0, the discount would be 32% off and if it's 30, the discount is only 2% off.

The idea was brilliant! The colder it got the more people would come in. We're able to make the cold work to our customers' advantage.

While the traditional Frozen Code is rumored to hold a complex series of calculations that the very first gelateri used to create perfect gelato, our senior assistant visiting anthropologist has derived fragments of the legendary code into a single calculation that can be used only in winter when the temperature is below 32 degrees.

One of the funniest things about it has been that a lot of kids from Bowdoin come in on cold winter nights. They will wait until 10:45, right before closing to get the coldest possible temperature. People will say they can't wait for "the Frozen" to kick in. It almost makes winter worth it. When it's really hot out in the summertime, people say it's a good thing that the code doesn't work in reverse and we charge extra for every degree over 32.

WILD MAINE BLUEBERRY CRISP

What could be more traditional here in Maine than a good blueberry crisp? Josh (whose family was all too familiar with "ku-plink, ku-plank, ku-plunk" when he was little) was inspired by a well-worn Marjorie Standish cookbook when creating this flavor. We create a tasty vanilla bean gelato, swirl in lots of wild blueberries from Down East, and top with our oat streusel. It's creamy with lots of blueberry bursts and a sweet crunch.

This gelato was featured in *Bon Appetit; O, The Oprah Magazine;* and *Food & Wine.*

INGREDIENTS:

4 cups (32 oz. or 907g) Classic White Gelato Base

2 teaspoons (10g) pure vanilla extract

1 cup (6 oz. or 170g) Maine Wild Blueberry variegate

1 cup (6 oz. or 170g) Oat Crisp Topping

In a large bowl whisk together the Classic White Gelato Base, and vanilla until mixture is smooth and uniform in color. Place in a covered container and refrigerate until cold, 2 hours or overnight. Place the blueberry variegate and crisp topping separately in covered containers in the freezer. Chill a 2-quart metal bowl in the freezer.

Once the base has chilled, churn it in your home ice cream maker. When the gelato is done freezing scoop gelato into the cold bowl. Add the cold blueberry swirl and a sprinkle of oat topping and fold together so there are ribbons of berries. Do not over mix. Sprinkle extra oat topping on top. Cover and return bowl to the freezer.

Yield: 36 oz. (about 3 pints)

- -

WILD MAINE BLUEBERRIES AND CREAM

INGREDIENTS:

3¼ cups (26 oz. or 737g) Classic White Gelato Base

1½ cups (12 oz. or 340g) fresh or frozen wild Maine blueberries

¼ cup (1½ oz. or 42g) powdered sugar

1 tablespoon (14g) vanilla extract

In a blender, combine 1 cup Classic White Base, blueberries, and powdered sugar. Add the remaining Classic White Base and vanilla, blending until mixture is smooth and uniform in color. Place in a covered container and refrigerate until cold, 4 hours or overnight.

Once the base has chilled, churn it in your home ice cream maker.

Yield: 39 oz. (about 3 pints)

EXPLORATION AND DISCOVERY

Food and service should not be a static experience. We explore tastes, people, and culture with a spirit of discovery and within the parameters of the pursuit of excellence.

Sorbetto

Sorbetto flavors were originally served in southern Italy. At Gelato Fiasco we use water instead of cream, and the flavor comes directly from the amazing fruits or cocoa. Folks often think that they're like desserts marked "sorbet" in the grocery store—but then they realize that our flavors are so much more. At Gelato Fiasco, sorbetto flavors are dairy-free and typically appropriate for guests with vegan diets.

Important Note: Chunks are not your friends! They make for icy sorbetto! :(

ᏚAPPLE CIDERᏚ

INGREDIENTS:

1½ cups (12 oz. or 340g) fresh apple cider

1 cup (8 oz. or 227g) no sugar added apple-sauce

1⅜ cups (15 oz. or 425g) Sugar Syrup

½ cup (4 oz. or 113g) water

2 tablespoons (1 oz. or 28g) fresh lemon juice

¼ teaspoon (½g) ground cinnamon

½ teaspoon sea salt (3g)

Using a food processor, blender, or immersion blender, combine the cider, apple sauce, and sugar syrup. Add the water, lemon juice, cinnamon, and salt. Continue to blend until the mixture is silky smooth. Chill the mixture 30 minutes or overnight.

Once the base has chilled, churn it in your home ice cream maker.

Yield: 40 oz. (about 3 pints)

• •

ᏚAPPLE PIEᏚ

Around here you can have your pie and freeze it too! Add in some Candied Bacon to walk on the wild side.

INGREDIENTS:

1½ cups (12 oz. or 340g) fresh apple cider

1 cup (8 oz. or 227g) no sugar added apple-sauce

1⅜ cups (15 oz. or 425g) Sugar Syrup

½ cup (4 oz. or 113g) water

2 tablespoons (1 oz. or 28g) fresh lemon juice

½ teaspoon (1g) ground cinnamon

¼ teaspoon (½g) ground ginger

⅛ teaspoon (¼g) ground allspice

⅛ teaspoon (¼g) ground cloves

½ teaspoon (3g) sea salt

Using a food processor, blender, or immersion blender, combine the cider, applesauce, and sugar syrup. Add the water, lemon juice, cinnamon, ginger, all-spice, cloves, and salt. Continue to blend until the mixture is silky smooth. Chill the mixture 30 minutes or overnight.

Once the base has chilled, churn it in your home ice cream maker.

Yield: 40 oz. (about 3 pints)

APRICOT

We've heard it's good luck if you dream about apricots. Soft, sweet, mellow and a little tart, this sorbetto is definitely the stuff dreams are made of. Top it with some caramel or a drizzle of chocolate ganache for extra indulgence!

INGREDIENTS:

3 cups (16 oz. or 454g) very ripe fresh or frozen apricots, peeled, pitted, and pureed

1⅜ cups (15 oz. or 425g) Sugar Syrup

1⅛ cups (9 oz. or 255g) water

1 tablespoon (½ oz. or 14g) fresh lemon juice

½ teaspoon sea salt (3g)

Wash, dry and remove any peels, stems, leaves, pits or seeds from your fruit. Chop or cut your fruit into ¼-inch or 1-cm pieces. Using a food processor, blender, or immersion blender, puree the fruit and sugar syrup. Add the water, lemon juice, and salt. Continue to blend until the mixture is silky smooth. Chill the mixture 30 minutes or overnight.

Once the base has chilled, churn it in your home ice cream maker.

Yield: 41 oz. (about 3 pints)

AVOCADO PEACH

The texture is impossibly smooth and the taste combination of avocado and peach has to be experienced at least once in your life.

INGREDIENTS:

2½ cups (12 oz. or 340g) very ripe fresh or frozen peaches, pureed

1 peeled and pitted (4 oz. or 113g) avocado

1¼ cups (14 oz. or 397g) Sugar Syrup

1 cup (8 oz. or 227g) water

2 tablespoons (1 oz. or 14g) fresh lime juice

¾ teaspoon (5g) sea salt

Wash, dry, and remove any peels or pits from your fruit. Chop or cut the peaches and avocado into ¼-inch or 1-cm pieces. Using a food processor, blender, or immersion blender, puree the fruit and sugar syrup. Add the water, lime juice, and salt. Continue to blend until the mixture is silky smooth. Chill the mixture 30 minutes or overnight.

Once the base has chilled, churn it in your home ice cream maker.

Yield: 39 oz. (about 3 pints)

❦ BANANA ❧

Pure and clean, this banana sorbetto is the closest cross between fresh fruit and frozen dessert.

INGREDIENTS:

3 cups (16 oz. or 454g) very ripe fresh or frozen bananas, pureed

1¼ cups (14 oz. or 397g) Sugar Syrup

1¼ cups (10 oz. or 283g) water

1 tablespoon (½ oz. or 14g) fresh lemon juice

½ teaspoon sea salt (3g)

Wash, dry and remove any peels from your banana. Chop or cut your fruit into ¼-inch or 1-cm pieces. Using a food processor, blender, or immersion blender, puree the fruit and sugar syrup. Add the water, lemon juice and salt. Continue to blend until the mixture is silky smooth. Chill the mixture 30 minutes or overnight.

Once the base has chilled, churn it in your home ice cream maker.

Yield: 40 oz. (about 3 pints)

❦ BLACKBERRY ❧

Fresh blackberries are packed with tiny seeds. In this recipe, you'll need to blend and strain the fruit puree to remove the seeds; then add back the water to formulate the correct weight. In the shop we say, "That blackberry flavor you crave, minus the thorns and purple fingers!" Making it at home, you may come away with a couple of purple pinkies.

INGREDIENTS:

3 cups (16 oz. or 454g) very ripe fresh or frozen blackberries, pureed with 1 cup (8oz or 227g) water

1½ cups (16 oz. or 454g) Sugar Syrup

1 cup (8 oz. or 227g) water

1 tablespoon (½ oz. or 14g) fresh lemon juice

½ teaspoon sea salt (3g)

Wash, dry, and remove any stems, or leaves from your fruit. Combine blackberries with water and blend. Strain your blackberry mixture, saving the seeds in separate container. Weigh the seeds and add water equal to half the weight of the seeds. Blend and strain again. Double strained mixture should weigh 24 ounces (680g); if it's less, add water to bring it to 24 ounces (680g).

Using a food processor, blender, or immersion blender, puree the strained fruit and sugar syrup. Add the additional 8 ounces of water, lemon juice, and salt. Continue to blend until the mixture is silky smooth. Chill the mixture 30 minutes or overnight.

Once the base has chilled, churn it in your home ice cream maker.

Yield: 48 oz. (about 3+ pints)

⟪ BLOOD ORANGE ⟫

They say the earliest Fiascans picked blood oranges on the slopes of Mt. Vesuvius and hand-squeezed them to make this flavor extra special. The hues of each blood orange vary from fruit to fruit, but overall the glistening crimson juice will absolutely burst with visual, olfactory and gustatory delight!

INGREDIENTS:

2¼ cups (18 oz. or 567g) blood orange juice or puree

1¼ cups (14 oz. or 397g) Sugar Syrup

1¼ cups (10 oz. or 283g) water

1 tablespoon (½ oz or 14g) fresh lemon juice

½ teaspoon sea salt (3g)

Using a food processor, blender, or immersion blender combine the blood orange puree and sugar syrup. Add the water, lemon juice, and salt. Continue to blend until the mixture is silky smooth. Chill the mixture 30 minutes or overnight.

Once the base has chilled, churn it in your home ice cream maker.

Yield: 40 oz. (about 3 pints)

❧ BLUEBERRY COCONUT ☙

INGREDIENTS:

2½ cups (12 oz. or 340g) very ripe fresh or frozen wild Maine blueberries, pureed

1 can (~15 oz. or 425g) Goya coconut cream

½ cup (6 oz. or 170g) Sugar Syrup

1 cup (8 oz. or 227g) water

1 tablespoon (¾ oz. or 14g) fresh lime juice

½ teaspoon sea salt (3g)

Wash, dry, and remove any stems, or leaves, from your berries. Using a food processor, blender, or immersion blender, puree the blueberries, coconut cream and sugar syrup. Add the water, lime juice, and salt. Continue to blend until the mixture is silky smooth. Chill the mixture 30 minutes or overnight.

Once the base has chilled, churn it in your home ice cream maker.

Yield: 42 oz. (about 3 pints)

⦗ BLUEBERRY MOJITO ⦘

INGREDIENTS:

¼ cup (3g) fresh mint leaves

2 cups (10 oz. or 283g) very ripe fresh or
    frozen Maine wild blueberries, pureed

1 ½ cups (16 oz. or 454g) Sugar Syrup

1 cup (8 oz. or 227g) water

¼ cup (2 oz. or 57g) Meyer's dark rum

1 tablespoon (½ oz or 14g) fresh lemon juice

½ teaspoon sea salt (3g)

Wash, dry, and remove any stems, or leaves, from your blueberries. Using a food processor, blender, or immersion blender, puree the mint and sugar syrup. Add the blueberries, water, rum, lemon juice and salt. Continue to blend until the mixture is silky smooth. Chill the mixture 30 minutes or overnight.

Once the base has chilled, churn it in your home ice cream maker.

Yield: 36 oz. (about 3 pints)

⦗ CHAMPAGNE ⦘

Raise your dish to this elegant sorbetto. Choose your favorite bubbly, then clink your red spoons just like Thurston Howell III and Lovey did!

INGREDIENTS:

2½ cups (20 oz. or 624g) champagne

1 cup (12 oz. or 340g) Sugar Syrup

¾ cup (6 oz. or 170g) water

Pinch of sea salt (2g)

Using a food processor, blender, or immersion blender combine the champagne and sugar syrup. Add the water and salt. Continue to blend until the mixture is silky smooth. Chill the mixture 30 minutes or overnight.

Once the base has chilled, churn it in your home ice cream maker.

Yield: 38 oz. (about 3 pints)

ϾCIDER AND DOUGHNUTSϿ

Fresh from Maine orchards, crisp apple cider pairs with Frosty's or Holy Donut doughnuts in our shops. When making this at home, find the best cider and freshest doughnuts to make this autumn treat.

INGREDIENTS:

2½ cups (20 oz. or 567g) apple cider

1⅓ cups (15 oz. or 425g) Sugar Syrup

½ cup (4 oz. or 113g) water

½ teaspoon (1g) ground cinnamon

2 tablespoons (1 oz. or 28g) fresh lemon juice

Pinch of sea salt (or 2 g)

5 oz. (142g) doughnuts, chopped into ½-inch chunks (our cake doughnut holes were two pieces per ounce so we used 10)

3 tablespoons (2 oz. or 57g) Sugar Syrup

Using a food processor, blender, or immersion blender, combine the apple cider, 13 ounces of sugar syrup, water, cinnamon, lemon juice, and salt. Place in a covered container and refrigerate until cold, 4 hours or overnight.

Put the chopped doughnuts into a zip top plastic bag. Pour in the remaining 2 ounces of sugar syrup and shake the bag until the pieces of doughnut are coated. Close the zip top bag, pressing out as much air as you can. Place it and a 2-quart metal bowl in the freezer to chill.

Once the base has chilled, churn it in your home ice cream maker. When the sorbetto is done freezing, scoop it into the cold bowl. Add the sugar syrup coated doughnut pieces and fold together. Once combined put a lid on the stainless steel bowl and return it to the freezer.

Yield: 47 oz. (about 3 pints)

❧ CINNAMON PEAR ❧

The delicate flavor of pear is courted by tantalizing cinnamon. Did you know there are 3,000 varieties of pears worldwide? We love Anjou for this sorbetto: light and sweet, it goes hand in hand with the earthy cinnamon.

INGREDIENTS:

3 cups (16 oz. or 454g) very ripe fresh pears, peeled and seeded

1 ½ cups (16 oz. or 454g) Sugar Syrup

1 cup (8 oz. or 227g) water

1 teaspoon (2g) ground cinnamon

1 tablespoon (½ oz or 14g) fresh lemon juice

½ teaspoon (3g) sea salt

Wash, dry, and remove any peels, stems, or seeds from your pears. Chop or cut them into ¼-inch or 1-cm pieces. Using a food processor, blender, or immersion blender, puree the pears and sugar syrup. Add the water, cinnamon, lemon juice, and salt. Continue to blend until the mixture is silky smooth. Chill the mixture 30 minutes or overnight.

Once the base has chilled, churn it in your home ice cream maker.

Yield: 40 oz. (about 3 pints)

• •

❧ COCONUT; TOASTED COCONUT; OR COCONUT LIME

Whether sprinkled with toasted coconut, kissed with lime, or left on its own, this is a rich and dreamy sorbetto. We use Goya-brand coconut milk and coconut cream. It has the perfect amount of fat to sugar ratio that makes this recipe work. If you can't find Goya you may need to add a bit more coconut cream to give it the same creamy texture.

INGREDIENTS:

1 can (~13½ oz. or 383g) Goya coconut cream

1 can (~13½ oz. or 383g) Goya coconut milk

⅝ cup (7 oz. or 198g) Sugar Syrup

¾ cup (6 oz. or 170g) water

1 tablespoon (½ oz or 14g) fresh lemon juice or fresh lime juice for coconut lime sorbetto

Pinch of sea salt (2g)

Optional toasted coconut for sprinkling

Using a food processor, blender, or immersion blender, puree the coconut cream, coconut milk, and sugar syrup. Add the water, lemon juice and salt. Continue to blend until the mixture is silky smooth. Chill the mixture 30 minutes or overnight.

Once the base has chilled, churn it in your home ice cream maker.

Yield: 40 oz. (about 3 pints)

ALMOND BUTTER
CHOCOLATE CHUNK
GELATO

BLOOD ORANGE
SORBETTO

BLUEBERRY
RASPBERRY
SORBETTO

BROWNIE BATTER
GELATO

CAKE BATTER
GELATO

CARAMEL SEA SALT
GELATO

CARDAMOM
GELATO

CHOCOLATE
COOKIE DOUGH
GELATO

COOKIE DOUGH
GELATO

COOKIE THERAPY
GELATO

DARK CHOCOLATE
CARAMEL SEA SALT
GELATO

DARK CHOCOLATE
NOIR
SORBETTO

ESPRESSO CHIP
GELATO

ESPRESSO FIASCO
GELATO

HONEY GRAHAM
GELATO

HOUSE CHOCOLATE
GELATO

KIT KAT
GELATO

LICK AT ME, I'M THE
KING OF NEW YORK
GELATO

MADAGASCAR
VANILLA BEAN
GELATO

MAINE WILD
BLUEBERRY CRISP
GELATO

MILK CHOCOLATE
COVERED PRETZEL
GELATO

MINT COOKIES AND
CREAM
GELATO

MINT CHOCOLATE
CHUNK
GELATO

NETFLIX AND CHILL
GELATO

PASSIONFRUIT
SORBETTO

PEANUT BUTTER CUP
GELATO

PEANUT BUTTER
STRACCIATELLA
GELATO

PURE LEMON
SORBETTO

PURE LIME
SORBETTO

RASPBERRY TRUFFLE
SORBETTO

RIPE MANGO
SORBETTO

STRAWBERRY
BALSAMIC
SORBETTO

STRAWBERRY
GELATO

STRACCIATELLA
GELATO

TOASTED COCONUT
GELATO

CRANBERRY ORANGE

INGREDIENTS:

2 cups (16 oz. or 454g) fresh squeezed orange juice

1½ cups fresh cranberries or 1 cup (5 oz. or 142g) cranberry puree

1¼ cups (14 oz. or 397g) Sugar Syrup

¾ cup (6 oz. or 170g) water

1 tablespoon (½ oz. or 14g) fresh lemon juice

Pinch of sea salt (or 2 g)

Using a food processor, blender, or immersion blender, puree the orange juice, cranberry puree and sugar syrup. Add the water, lemon juice and salt. Continue to blend until the mixture is silky smooth. Chill the mixture 30 minutes or overnight.

Once the base has chilled, churn it in your home ice cream maker.

Yield: 41 oz. (about 3 pints)

• •

CUCUMBER LIME CILANTRO

INGREDIENTS:

2 cups (12 oz. or 340g) peeled, seeded, cucumbers

2 tablespoons (2g) chopped fresh cilantro

½ cup (4 oz. or 113g) fresh lime juice

1½ cups (16 oz. or 454g) Sugar Syrup

1¼ cup (10 oz. or 283g) water

½ teaspoon (3g) sea salt

Wash, dry, and remove any peels, and seeds from your cucumbers. Chop or cut your fruit into ¼-inch or 1-cm pieces. Using a food processor, blender, or immersion blender, puree the cucumber, cilantro, lime juice, and sugar syrup. Add the water and salt. Continue to blend until the mixture is silky smooth. Chill the mixture 30 minutes or overnight.

Once the base has chilled, churn it in your home ice cream maker.

Yield: 42 oz. (about 3 pints)

GOLDEN MELON

Look for a melon that's firm with a slight give to the rind and has a glorious fragrance, eager to reveal the secret sweetness inside.

INGREDIENTS:

3 cups (16 oz. or 454g) very ripe fresh, canta-loupe melon, without seeds or rind

1 ½ cups (16 oz. or 454g) Sugar Syrup

1 cup (8 oz. or 227g) water

1 tablespoon (½ oz. or 14g) fresh lemon juice

½ teaspoon sea salt (3g)

Wash, dry and remove any rind or seeds from your cantaloupe. Chop or cut the melon into ¼-inch or 1-cm pieces. Using a food processor, blender, or immersion blender, puree the fruit and sugar syrup. Add the water, lemon juice, and salt. Continue to blend until the mixture is silky smooth. Chill the mixture 30 minutes or overnight.

Once the base has chilled, churn it in your home ice cream maker.

Yield: 40 oz. (about 3 pints)

• •

GRAPEFRUIT

INGREDIENTS:

2½ cups (20 oz. or 624g) pure grapefruit juice, white, pink, or red

1½ cups (16 oz. or 454g) Sugar Syrup

⅔ cup (5 oz. or 227g) water

1 tablespoon (½ oz. or 14g) fresh lemon juice

½ teaspoon sea salt (3g)

Using a food processor, blender, or immersion blender, combine the grapefruit juice and sugar syrup. Add the water, lemon juice and salt. Continue to blend until the mixture is silky smooth. Chill the mixture 30 minutes or overnight.

Once the base has chilled, churn it in your home ice cream maker.

Yield: 41 oz. (about 3 pints)

❧ HARD CIDER ❧

INGREDIENTS:

2½ cups (20 oz. or 624g) hard cider

1⅛ cups (13 oz. or 369g) Sugar Syrup

¾ cup (6 oz. or 170g) water

Pinch of sea salt (or 2 g)

Using a food processor, blender, or immersion blender, combine the hard cider and sugar syrup. Add the water, and salt. Continue to blend until the mixture is silky smooth. Chill the mixture 30 minutes or overnight.

Once the base has chilled, churn it in your home ice cream maker.

Yield: 39 oz. (about 3 pints)

• •

❧ HEIRLOOM TOMATO ❧

Yes, really . . . tomato . . . sorbetto. Tomato is a fruit after all. The sorbetto becomes the perfect palate cleanser and a light, delicate dessert. Drizzling with a balsamic reduction is blissful.

INGREDIENTS:

3 cups (16 oz. or 454g) very ripe fresh heirloom tomato, peeled, and seeded

1½ cups (16 oz. or 454g) Sugar Syrup

1 cup (8 oz. or 227g) water

1 tablespoon (½ oz. or 14g) fresh lemon juice

½ teaspoon sea salt (3g)

Wash, dry, and remove the peels, stems, leaves, cores, and seeds from your tomatoes—be sure to remove all of the seeds as they are especially bitter. Chop or cut the tomato into ¼-inch or 1-cm pieces. Using a food processor, blender, or immersion blender, puree the tomato and sugar syrup. Add the water, lemon juice, and salt. Continue to blend until the mixture is silky smooth. Chill the mixture 30 minutes or overnight.

Once the base has chilled, churn it in your home ice cream maker.

Yield: 40 oz. (about 3 pints)

❦ HIBISCUS LEMONADE ❧

Gorgeous ruby hues tint sweet and sour lemon sorbetto. The floral tea transforms the pucker into a beatific smile.

INGREDIENTS:

¾ cup (6 oz. or 170g) fresh lemon juice

2 cups (16 oz. or 454g) brewed hibiscus tea

1⅝ cups (18 oz. or 567g) Sugar Syrup

Pinch of sea salt (or 2 g)

Using a food processor, blender, or immersion blender, combine the lemon juice, tea, sugar syrup, and salt. Continue to blend until the mixture is silky smooth. Chill the mixture 30 minutes or overnight.

Once the base has chilled, churn it in your home ice cream maker.

Yield: 40 oz. (about 3 pints)

• •

❦ FRESH LIME ❧

INGREDIENTS:

¾ cup (6 oz. or 170g) fresh lime juice

1¾ cups (19 oz. or 595g) Sugar Syrup

1⅞ cups (15 oz. or 425g) water

Pinch of sea salt (or 2 g)

Using a food processor, blender, or immersion blender, combine the lime juice and sugar syrup. Add the water, and salt. Continue to blend until the mixture is silky smooth. Chill the mixture 30 minutes or overnight.

Once the base has chilled, churn it in your home ice cream maker.

Yield: 40 oz. (about 3 pints)

⚜ RIPE MANGO ⚜

No mango trees around these parts, but a Mainer can dream, right? Every snowy February, we jet out of PWM to somewhere warm and tropical. The rest of the year, this seductive sorbetto—which they say tastes like the islands—does the trick. Don't forget your sunscreen!

Ripe Mango Sorbetto won the 2016 sofi Award from the Specialty Food Association for Outstanding Ice Cream, Gelato, or Frozen Treat. It was also featured in the August 2015 issue of *O: The Oprah Magazine* as an editors' pick. The quote from *O* was, "You can't buy happiness but you can buy this rich and satiny Maine made gelato and that's pretty darn close."

INGREDIENTS:

3 cups (16 oz. or 454g) very ripe fresh or frozen mango, pureed

1½ cups (16 oz. or 454g) Sugar Syrup

1 cup (8 oz. or 227g) water

1 tablespoon (½ oz. or 14g) fresh lemon juice

½ teaspoon sea salt (3g)

Wash, dry, and remove any peels, stems, or pits from your mango. Chop or cut your fruit into ¼-inch or 1-cm pieces. Using a food processor, blender, or immersion blender, puree the mango and sugar syrup. Add the water, lemon juice, and salt. Continue to blend until the mixture is silky smooth. Chill the mixture 30 minutes or overnight.

Once the base has chilled, churn it in your home ice cream maker.

Yield: 40 oz. (about 3 pints)

⤲ WILD MAINE BLUEBERRY ⤳

We only make this in August because Bruno will only allow us to make it with fresh blueberries. It really does make difference. Make sure your fresh fruit is as ripe as possible. Riper fruit tastes sweeter and blends easier.

INGREDIENTS:

3 cups (16 oz. or 454g) very ripe fresh or frozen wild Maine blueberries, pureed

1½ cups (16 oz. or 454g) Sugar Syrup

1 cup (8 oz. or 227g) water

1 tablespoon (½ oz. or 14g) fresh lemon juice

½ teaspoon sea salt (3g)

Wash, dry, and remove any stems or leaves from your blueberries. Using a food processor, blender, or immersion blender, puree the fruit and sugar syrup. Add the water, lemon juice, and salt. Continue to blend until the mixture is silky smooth. Chill the mixture 30 minutes or overnight.

Once the base has chilled, churn it in your home ice cream maker.

Yield: 40 oz. (about 3 pints)

❦ SUPER BERRY ❧

Sorbetto with all of the berries. This blend of summer sunshine is a basket bursting with flavor.

INGREDIENTS:

1 heaping cup (6 oz. or 170g) very ripe fresh or frozen strawberries, pureed

¾ cup (3 oz. or 85g) very ripe fresh or frozen blueberries, pureed

1 cup (4 oz. or 113g) raspberry puree

1 cup (3 oz. or 85g) very ripe fresh or frozen blackberries, pureed

1⅜ cups (15 oz. or 425g) Sugar Syrup

1 tablespoon (½ oz. or 14g) fresh lemon juice

Pinch of sea salt (or 2 g)

Wash, dry, and remove any stems or leaves from your berries. Chop or cut your strawberries into ¼-inch or 1-cm pieces. Using a food processor, blender, or immersion blender, puree all of the berries and sugar syrup. Add the lemon juice and salt. Continue to blend until the mixture is silky smooth. Chill the mixture 30 minutes or overnight.

Once the base has chilled, churn it in your home ice cream maker.

Yield: 40 oz. (about 3 pints)

• •

❦ MOXIE (OR ROOTBEER) ❧

Courageous, daring, spirited… that guy's got Moxie! Not for the faint of heart, Moxie is an old school rootbeer-esque soda that many Mainers were weaned on. The earthy, complex flavor was once a tonic to cure what ails ya. Now it's just delicious! (Of course, if you're one of those who just hasn't taken a shine to Moxie, you can substitute with root beer.)

INGREDIENTS:

3 cups (24 oz. or 680g) Moxie or Rootbeer

1⅓ cups (14 oz. or 397g) Sugar Syrup

½ cup (4 oz. or 113g) water

Pinch of sea salt (or 2 g)

Using a food processor, blender, or immersion blender, combine the Moxie and sugar syrup. Add the water, and salt. Continue to blend until the mixture is homogenous. Chill the mixture 30 minutes or overnight.

Once the base has chilled, churn it in your home ice cream maker.

Yield: 42 oz. (about 3 pints)

⸻ DARK CHOCOLATE NOIR ⸻

Our truly dense, dark, "oh-my" chocolate sorbetto was created by Bruno in response to a pro chef's challenge. He still comes in regularly to buy it for his restaurant! We hope it will make you happy, too.

INGREDIENTS:

2½ cups (7½ oz. or 212g) cocoa powder

1¾ cups (18 oz. or 567g) Sugar Syrup

1⅞ cup (15 oz. or 425g) water

Pinch of sea salt (or 2g)

Using a food processor, blender, or immersion blender, combine the cocoa powder and sugar syrup. Add the water, and salt. Continue to blend until the mixture is silky smooth. Chill the mixture 30 minutes or overnight.

Once the base has chilled, churn it in your home ice cream maker.

Yield: 40 oz. (about 3 pints)

⸻ OLD MAJOR PERSNICKETY'S CURE ⸻ FOR THE COMMON COLD

THE LEGEND

Old Major Persnickety had but one job: to guard the ice. The Secretary of War had ordered a strategic ice supply to be held, even in peacetime, and it was Persnickety's job to protect it. It was a calling that required vigilance, several layers of clothing, and constant shuffling. But things had a tendency to get chilly and Old Major was prone to catching colds (even when they said that the cold doesn't actually cause colds).

After a few rounds of this, our protagonist tried for months—nay, years!—to figure out how to ward off the phlegmatory unpleasantness. He tried juicing, he mixed spices, he spent all his Polar Points on orange powders. One day, leafing through his moleskin of ingredients and equations, he had a brain wave (that's the opposite of a brain freeze): some vitamin-rich citrus, some immune-boosting honey, some digestive-healing ginger, and some whiskey (no reason was deduced for that part). It became then, is now, and will always be, his cure for the common cold.

POST SCRIPT

But Persnickety's perfection would not be known to us today if not for a delightful twist of fate. Just about the time that the Gold Standard was abolished, it was decided that the Ice Reserve was a relic. So Old Major was left to collect his pension and retire, and he set off to the Belgrade Lakes region of Maine, a place where he thought no one would be a bother.

But a short distance from his cabin sat the home of Charlie and Margie, whose son, Joshua, had a penchant for business and a preference for mischief. One day, Old Major was sitting on his porch when Joshua wandered through the yard in search of acorns that he planned to offer as "hand-foraged, natural artisanal hot nuts" at the farmer's market. The jovial and loquacious boy spotted Old Major and just wouldn't stop talking.

Feeling that the nut plan was a bit squirrely, Persnickety aimed to change the conversation and started telling Joshua fantastic, if embellished, stories about his decades at the Reserve. Over that visit, and many uninvited but accommodated future visits on that porch, Joshua learned of the Teapot Cube Scandal, the Tray-Packing Scheme, a legendary "Frozen Code" that was discussed among men who shipped ice, and finally, greatly, most astonishingly, Persnickety's recipe to cure any cold. That recipe stayed with Joshua for many years, and finally takes shape today, with Persnickety long remembered, in the sorbetto that bears his sole triumph and his most memorable name.

INGREDIENTS:

1½ cups (12 oz. or 340g) fresh orange juice

1 cup (8 oz. or 227g) fresh lemon juice

1 cup plus 1 tablespoon (12 oz. or 340g) Sugar Syrup

¼ cup (2½ oz. or 71g) honey

1 cup (8 oz or 227g) water

½ teaspoon (2g) ground ginger

¼ teaspoon (1g) cayenne pepper

2 tablespoons (1 oz. or 28g) Wild Turkey bourbon

Pinch of sea salt (or 2g)

In a large bowl, combine the orange juice, lemon juice, sugar syrup, honey, water, ginger, cayenne, bourbon, and salt. Whisk until the mixture is very smooth and the honey is dissolved. Chill the mixture 30 minutes or overnight.

Once the base has chilled, churn it in your home ice cream maker.

Yield: 44 oz. (about 3 pints)

❦ PEACH MELBA ❧

The history of Peach Melba involves a chef, an opera singer, a swan, and heartfelt appreciation for art and beauty. Succulent ripe peaches marry crimson raspberry puree for this sweet and tart sorbetto.

INGREDIENTS:

2 cups (12 oz. or 340g) very ripe fresh or frozen peaches, pureed

1 cup (4 oz. or 113g) raspberry puree

1½ cups (15 oz. or 425g) Sugar Syrup

1 cup plus 2 tablespoons (9 oz. or 255g) water

1 tablespoon (½ oz. or 14g) fresh lemon juice

Pinch of sea salt (or 2g)

Wash, dry, and remove any peels, leaves, or pits from your peaches. Chop or cut the peaches into ¼-inch or 1-cm pieces. Using a food processor, blender, or immersion blender, puree the peaches, raspberries, and sugar syrup. Add the water, lemon juice, and salt. Continue to blend until the mixture is silky smooth. Chill the mixture 30 minutes or overnight.

Once the base has chilled, churn it in your home ice cream maker.

Yield: 40 oz. (about 3 pints)

• •

❦ PINEAPPLE ❧

There is a famous theme park that serves a frozen pineapple swirly business. Juicy and tangy, this sorbetto brings the fresh fruit to new, sweet, dizzying heights!

INGREDIENTS:

2 cups (16 oz. or 454g) very ripe fresh or frozen pineapple chunks, pureed

1½ cups (15 oz. or 425g) Sugar Syrup

1¼ cups (10 oz. or 227g) water

1 tablespoon (½ oz. or 14g) fresh lemon juice

Pinch of sea salt (or 2g)

Wash, dry, and remove any peels, stems, seeds, or core from your pineapple. Chop or cut your fruit into ¼-inch or 1-cm pieces. Using a food processor, blender, or immersion blender, puree the pineapple and sugar syrup. Add the water, lemon juice, and salt. Continue to blend until the mixture is silky smooth. Chill the mixture 30 minutes or overnight.

Once the base has chilled, churn it in your home ice cream maker.

Yield: 41 oz. (about 3 pints)

PINEAPPLE CASHEW COCONUT

The toasty nuts give this sorbetto a welcome crunch in what tastes like an extra frosty island drink. A scoop of this drizzled with dark rum would make a decadent dessert... sarong not required!

INGREDIENTS:

1¼ cup (10 oz. or 283g) very ripe fresh or frozen pineapple chunks, pureed

1 can (13½ oz. or 383g) Goya coconut cream

⅔ cup (6 oz. or 170g) Sugar Syrup

1¼ cups (10 oz. or 283g) water

1 tablespoon (½ oz. or 14g) fresh lime juice

Pinch of sea salt (or 2g)

¾ cup (4 oz. or 113g) roasted cashews, chopped

Wash, dry, and remove any skin/rind, leaves, or core from your pineapple. Chop or cut your fruit into ¼-inch or 1-cm pieces. Using a food processor, blender, or immersion blender, puree the pineapple, coconut cream, and sugar syrup. Add the water, lemon juice, and salt. Continue to blend until the mixture is silky smooth. Chill the mixture 30 minutes or overnight. Place the chopped roasted cashews in a zip top plastic bag. Set the bag and a 2-quart metal bowl to chill in the freezer.

Once the base has chilled, churn it in your home ice cream maker. Once the sorbetto is done freezing scoop it into the cold bowl. Add cold roasted cashews and fold together. Once combined cover the bowl and put in back in the freezer.

Yield: 43 oz. (about 3 pints)

❧ POMEGRANATE CHUNK ❧

Tart pomegranate makes a nice foil for the chocolate truffle chunks in this fan favorite. It was one of our original pint flavors and we constantly field requests to bring it back whenever it's out of season. Well, now you can have it any time at home!

INGREDIENTS:

1¼ cups (10 oz. or 283g) pomegranate juice

1 cup (7 oz. or 198g) cherry puree (see instructions to make your own)

1⅛ cup (14 oz. or 397g) Sugar Syrup

1⅛ cup (9 oz. or 255g) water

1 tablespoon (½ oz. or 14g) lemon juice

1 teaspoon (6g) sea salt

5 oz. roughly chopped Homemade Chocolate Truffle chunks or to taste

To Make the Cherry Puree: using a food processor, finely puree about 1 cup of either fresh or frozen pitted cherries that have been thawed. Let the machine run for a bit; you want it as smooth as possible.

In a large bowl whisk together the pomegranate juice, cherry puree, sugar syrup, water, lemon juice, and salt until mixture is smooth and uniform in color. Place in a covered container and refrigerate until cold, 4 hours or overnight. Place the chocolate chunks in a zip top plastic bag. Set the bag and a 2-quart metal bowl to chill in the freezer.

Once the base has chilled, churn it in your home ice cream maker. Once the sorbetto is done freezing scoop it into the cold bowl. Add cold chocolate chunks and fold together. Once combined cover the bowl and put in back in the freezer.

Yield: 45 oz. (about 3 pints)

❧ PURE LEMON ❧

This sorbetto is the perfect palate cleanser! Brings us back to sweltering hot summer days, riding our bikes down to the corner store and buying a quarter's worth of Italian ice. Lip puckering sour lemon, immediately soothed by the sweet chill of icy cold refreshment.

INGREDIENTS:

1 cup (8 oz. or 227g) fresh lemon juice

1¾ cups (18 oz. or 567g) Sugar Syrup

1¼ cups (14 oz. or 397 grams) water

Pinch of sea salt (or 2g)

Using a blender or immersion blender pulse the lemon juice and sugar syrup.

Add the water and salt. Continue to blend until the mixture is silky smooth. Chill the mixture 30 minutes or overnight.

Once the base has chilled, churn it in your home ice cream maker.

Yield: 40 oz. (about 3 pints)

❧ RASPBERRY LIME RICKEY ❧

This sorbetto is inspired by a classic summer drink our grandmothers might have shared with our grandfathers sitting side-by-side in a booth at the soda fountain. Two straws.

INGREDIENTS:

3 cups (12 oz. or 340g) fresh raspberries, pureed

½ cup (4 oz. or 113g) fresh lime juice

1½ cups (15 oz. or 425g) Sugar Syrup

1 cup (8 oz. or 227g) water

1 tablespoon (½ oz or 14g) fresh lemon juice

Pinch of sea salt (or 2 g)

Using a food processor, blender, or immersion blender puree the raspberries, lime juice, and sugar syrup. Add the water, lemon juice, and salt. Continue to blend until the mixture is silky smooth. Chill the mixture 30 minutes or overnight.

Once the base has chilled, churn it in your home ice cream maker.

Yield: 39 oz. (about 3 pints)

COMMUNITY SUPPORT

We help build the neighborhoods in which we live and work. In the past five years, we've partnered with more than fifty organizations and donated more than $65,000 back to the greater Brunswick and Portland communities.

ʒ RASPBERRY TRUFFLE ʒ

Chocolate chunks add texture and richness to a smooth red raspberry sorbetto.

INGREDIENTS:

4 cups (16 oz. or 454g) very ripe fresh or frozen red raspberries, pureed or macerated

1⅓ cups (14 oz. or 454g) Sugar Syrup

1 cup (10 oz. or 227 grams) water

1 tablespoon (½ oz. or 14 grams) fresh lemon juice

Pinch of sea salt (or 2 g)

¾ cup (4 oz. or 113g) Homemade Chocolate Truffle pieces or chocolate chips

Wash, dry and remove any stems or leaves from your raspberries. Using a food processor, blender, or immersion blender puree the raspberries and sugar syrup.

Add the water, lemon juice, and salt. Continue to blend until the mixture is silky smooth. Chill the mixture 30 minutes or overnight. Place the chocolate truffle pieces or chocolate chips in a zip top plastic bag in the freezer along with a covered metal bowl.

Once the base has chilled, churn it in your home ice cream maker. Once the sorbettto is done freezing, scoop it into the cold bowl. Add the cold chocolate and fold together. Once combined cover the bowl and return it to the freezer.

Yield: 44 oz. (about 3 pints)

⚬ SHISO MELON ⚬

Light and sweet, this sorbetto is like eating a creamier version of the real thing. The shiso leaves add an herbaceous citrus note that is a beautiful counterpoint to the clean, crisp melon.

INGREDIENTS:

About 9 (7g) chopped fresh shiso leaves

3 cups (16 oz. or 454g) chopped, fresh or frozen honeydew melon, rind removed and seeded

1½ cups (16 oz. or 454g) Sugar Syrup

1 cup (8 oz. or 227g) water

2 tablespoons (1 oz. or 28g) fresh lemon juice

Pinch of sea salt (or 2g)

Wash, dry, and remove the rind and seeds from your melon. Chop or cut your fruit into ¼-inch or 1-cm pieces. Using a food processor, blender, or immersion blender, puree the chopped shiso leaves and sugar syrup until smooth. Add the melon and blend until there are no chunks. Add the water, lemon juice, and salt. Continue to blend until the mixture is silky smooth. Chill the mixture 30 minutes or overnight.

Once the base has chilled, churn it in your home ice cream maker.

Yield: 40 oz. (about 3 pints)

✄STRAWBERRY BALSAMIC✄

Bruno learned from his Italian nonna that a touch of balsamico enhances the sweetness of ripe strawberries to perfection. This sorbetto confirms that Granny was right! Just down the street from our flagship store in Brunswick you'll find Fiore Artisan Olive Oils and Vinegars. They have partnered with a Maine wild blueberry grower to develop a gorgeous balsamic vinegar that celebrates this spectacular flavor! It perfectly suits the sweet tang of fresh strawberries in a marriage made in Maine!

INGREDIENTS:

3 cups (16 oz. or 454g) chopped, fresh or frozen strawberries- wild ones if you can find them

1 ½ cups (16 oz. or 454g) Sugar Syrup

1 cup (8 oz. or 227g) water

1 tablespoon (½ oz. or 14g) fresh lemon juice

1 tablespoon (½ oz. or 14g) balsamic vinegar

Pinch of sea salt (or 2 g)

Wash, dry, and remove any leaves from your berries. Chop or cut your fruit into ¼-inch or 1-cm pieces. Using a food processor, blender, or immersion blender, puree the fruit and sugar syrup. Add the water, lemon juice, balsamic vinegar, and salt. Continue to blend until the mixture is silky smooth. Chill the mixture 30 minutes or overnight.

Once the base has chilled, churn it in your home ice cream maker.

Yield: 40 oz. (about 3 pints)

❦ STRAWBERRY RHUBARB ❧

In Maine for sure, spring is heralded by Grandma's (or Memere's) homemade strawberry rhubarb pie, with a latticework crust carefully criss-crossing a tart and sweet filling. This sorbetto is our homage to the that wonderful pie filling. We twist our field-fresh strawberry balsamic recipe with stalks of rhubarb for a frozen treat that's only available during the gleeful period between spring and summer. If you'd like to take this sorbetto to the next level, fold in the Crisp Inclusion to add another texture and dimension to this summery treat.

INGREDIENTS:

2 cups (12 oz. or 340g) fresh strawberries— wild ones if you can find them

¾ cup (4 oz. or 113g) chopped fresh rhubarb

1½ cups (16 oz. or 454g) Sugar Syrup

1 cup (8 oz. or 227g) water

1 tablespoon (½ oz. or 14g) fresh lemon juice

Pinch of sea salt (or 2g)

(Optional: 1 cup (3 oz. or 85g) chilled Oat Crisp Topping)

Wash, dry, and remove any leaves or dirt from your fruit. Chop or cut your strawberries and rhubarb into ¼-inch or 1-cm pieces. Using a food processor, blender, or immersion blender, puree the fruit and sugar syrup. Add the water, lemon juice, and salt. Continue to blend until the mixture is silky smooth. Chill the mixture 30 minutes or overnight.

Once the base has chilled, churn it in your home ice cream maker. If you'd like to add the crisp inclusion, fold it in now, then transfer the sorbetto to a covered container and freeze until you're ready to serve.

Yield: 40 oz. (about 3 pints)

❦ SWEET CITRUS ❦

When making sorbetto from juice it's best to squeeze your own or find frozen-fresh purees. Fresh juice tastes closer to the fruit itself. This sorbetto is luscious sitting beside any vanilla gelato or coconut sorbetto. Together they taste like a creamsicle!

INGREDIENTS:

3 cups (24 oz. or 680g) fresh squeezed orange juice

1⅓ cups (15 oz. or 425g) Sugar Syrup

½ cup (4 oz. or 227g) water

2 tablespoons (1 oz. or 28g) fresh lemon juice

1 teaspoon (6g) sea salt

Using a food processor, blender, or immersion blender, combine the juice and sugar syrup. Add the water, lemon juice and salt. Continue to blend until the mixture is silky smooth. Chill the mixture 30 minutes or overnight.

Once the base has chilled, churn it in your home ice cream maker.

Yield: 44 oz. (about 3 pints)

• •

❦ WATERMELON ❦

When making watermelon sorbetto, you don't have to add any additional hydration. The fruit itself is full of moisture. The base with an extra squeeze of lemon makes a delightful, summer beverage! Add some frozen cubes of watermelon and its good enough to drink on its own!

INGREDIENTS:

4½ cups (24 oz. or 454g) very ripe watermelon, seeded, rind trimmed, cut into ½" (1cm) chunks

1½ cups (16 oz. or 454g) Sugar Syrup

1 tablespoon (½ oz. or 14g) fresh lemon juice

½ teaspoon sea salt (3g)

Wash, dry, and remove the layers of both green and white rind and seeds from the watermelon. Chop or cut it into ¼-inch or 1-cm pieces. Using a food processor, blender, or immersion blender, puree the fruit and sugar syrup. Add the lemon juice and salt. Continue to blend until the mixture is silky smooth. Chill the mixture 30 minutes or overnight.

Once the base has chilled, churn it in your home ice cream maker.

Yield: 40 oz. (about 3 pints)

OUR TRUE NORTH

When you own a storefront and have staff ready to serve, there's often the temptation to add additional items to the menu (The Legendary Toast, for instance) or to introduce a gift product selection. We've tried various things over the years . . . complex specialty coffee drinks, brownie sundaes, baked Aroostooks—our version of a baked Alaska, and much more. Those things are great, but you have to be careful that they don't pull staff away from guiding customers through a terrific gelato experience.

What we've learned, again and again, is that people really visit Gelato Fiasco for exceptional gelato and kind hospitality. So ten years in, that's where we try to keep our focus: making the best gelato available anywhere, and offering it alongside carefully considered items that definitively add to the experience, such as our fresh waffle cones and distinctive God of Thunder coffee. That's the focus that we hoped to share with you through this book—simple ingredients and thoughtful approaches that will help you make excellent desserts that will delight you, your friends, and family.

Today, Gelato Fiasco sells pints nationwide—all made in Maine at the Flavor Foundry. We have built this national footprint using the same recipes and ingredients we use in our shops here in Maine, making gelato the same way we always have. We've been lucky to be able to travel across the country telling people about Gelato Fiasco and convincing them to give us a shot. We're not the cheapest gelato on the shelf, but once people give us a try, they usually understand and become lifetime fans. In one of the most surreal parts of our lives so far, we even traveled to Australia to oversee the launch of Gelato Fiasco Down Under. It's truly been an unbelievable journey, and we're excited to see where gelato will bring us next.

SCOOPING FOR COMMUNITY

We believe that the most important role our shops play in our communities occurs through the sense of place they provide. Our stores are friendly, inclusive, and interesting spaces for people to gather. Great connections occur over gelato and coffee. People share, talk, and learn at our stores, and, we hope, build a sense of pride for a business made the Maine way.

Gelato Fiasco also supports important community organizations with direct financial support through our Scooping for Community Program. We partner with non-profits and donate 100% of sales from a non-profit's supporters on the organization's designated Scooping for Community Day. In the past five seasons, we've partnered with more than fifty organizations and donated more than $65,000 back to the greater Brunswick and Portland communities.

RED SPOON SOCIETY

The Red Spoon Society is Gelato Fiasco's elite rewards brother- and sister-hood that dates back to . . . "a very long time ago." New members who hope to join must fill out a petition for induction. Those chosen to enter the ranks have no responsibilities but enjoy many privileges. If you visit our Maine stores, you'll earn points for substantial rewards. If you're not from Maine and want to stay connected because you purchase our gelato at your local grocery store, you'll receive news, updates, and surprises. It's free to join and there is no card to carry or lose.

For centuries, members of the Red Spoon Society wove clues to their treasure of gelato secrets into some of history's most valuable works of art, commerce, and culture. These items were discovered by Josh and Bruno, and have been restored and preserved by Gelato Fiasco's anthropology and art history team. Some of these artworks and artifacts are on display at Gelato Fiasco's stores; other works remain in Gelato Fiasco's subterranean vault.

RECIPE INDEX